SAHARA

THUNDER BAY
P · R · E · S · S

San Diego, California

TEXT
PAOLO NOVARESIO

INTRODUCTION
ALBERTO SALZA

HISTORICAL INTRODUCTION
GIANNI GUADALUPI

EDITORIAL PROJECT
VALERIA MANFERTO DE FABIANIS

GRAPHIC DESIGN
CLARA ZANOTTI

EDITORIAL COORDINATION
LARA GIORCELLI
LAURA ACCOMAZZO

8 THE LEGENDARY TUAREG PROUDLY MAINTAIN THEIR ANCESTRAL CUSTOMS AND HERITAGE.

8–9 SOARING, SINUOUS SANDY RIDGES LIKE THIS ONE IN EGYPT ARE TYPICAL OF THE GREAT *ERGS*.

CONTENTS

INTRODUCTION   PAGE 10

THE DISCOVERY
OF THE SAHARA   PAGE 20

HORIZONS OF SAND   PAGE 58
SECRETS OF THE
MOUNTAINS   PAGE 104

THE ART OF SURVIVAL   PAGE 118

PROGENY OF THE SUN   PAGE 134
THE LARGEST MUSEUM
IN THE WORLD   PAGE 140

PEOPLES OF THE SAHARA PAGE 152

LIVING IN THE SAHARA   PAGE 216
FARMERS OF THE SAND   PAGE 224

CARAVANS AND THE
SALT ROADS   PAGE 240

PASTURELANDS   PAGE 256

DESERT CAPITALS   PAGE 274

Index   PAGE 296
Photo Credits   PAGE 299

10–11 A CARAVAN SEEKS THE EASIEST WAY THROUGH THE DUNES. IN THE LEEWARD AREAS, THE SAND IS OFTEN SO SOFT THAT IT CAN BARELY SUPPORT THE WEIGHT OF A DROMEDARY.

11 LEFT The Mauritanian Sahara seems to stretch on endlessly toward the heart of North Africa. The uniformity of the dunes is due to the sifting action of the wind, which makes the sand almost powdery.

11 RIGHT A cloud of sand rises from the crest of a dune in the Mauritanian desert, creating a surprisingly beautiful effect. The wind is the primary creator of the Saharan choreography.

INTRODUCTION

BY ALBERTO SALZA

The Sahara is nothing but a cliché. "It's a sea of sand," I said before my first crossing. After the soles of my shoes were torn apart by the sharp stones of the *hammadas* and my tires ripped on the tracks of the *tassilis,* I realized I was wrong. The fault lies with the photographers, who include soft sand dunes in 80 percent of their desert photographs. In reality, shifting mounds of sand cover less than 10 percent of the Sahara; the rest is a landscape of rocks more or less destroyed by erosion. The fact is that the dunes are photogenic, like the curves of a naked woman. And they are just as unapproachable. When traveling with the puritanical Islamic camel drivers, we took every possible precaution to stay away from the *ergs,* the seas of sand and dunes that cut off the path of caravans, sucking at

travelers' legs and leaving them breathless in a whirl of siliceous particles. When you're in the middle of the Sahara, the collective imagination seems to dissolve into sand in your eyes.

"In Wadi Halfa, in Sudan, at the extreme eastern edge of the Sahara, the temperature at ground level reaches 176 degrees Fahrenheit," I told Saleh, the caravan leader, one January evening. We were unloading the dromedaries, removing blocks of salt bound for Timbuktu. I was shaking with cold; the salt felt like ice. "The scientists measured it," I added, as if that fact had some relevance, there in the subzero void. "Words are like eggs," declared Saleh, huffing and puffing inside his veil. "As soon as they hatch, they grow wings. If you don't be quiet, your tongue will fall out. The *laialì* weather has begun, the cold that breaks the feet of the

dromedaries. Let's hurry." I was afraid. "In the Sahara, if the dromedary dies, you die," a Tuareg told me in Algeria. So I forgot about the cold and thought of the rain. It never rains in the Sahara, it is said, but I had almost drowned near In Salah when a wave of floodwater caught me by surprise in the channel of a wadi, a riverbed that had been dry for centuries in one of the hottest places in the Sahara. The Sahara is a vague, nebulous shape-shifter; things are never where and what they should be.

The Sahara does not even have a name: the word means something like "empty place," "abandoned," any desert where nothing living is supposed to be. But if you stop somewhere in the Sahara, in the nothingness, anyone in the vicinity will feel duty bound to meet you, perhaps going miles out of his way just to talk, or give you a hand, or drink tea, or simply gossip a little. It seems to be the law of the desert, the foundation for man's deep social instincts. *"Quand on est dans le dèsert, on est dans la mèrde,"* said a Tuareg I met, who had found a modern solution to the nomadic urges of his people by driving a truck through the web of roads between the oasis and the city.

Aside from people, the Sahara is teeming with life. One night we stopped near Laouni, near the Niger border. For once, no one appeared, apart from the ghosts of the Foreign Legion whose fort had once stood there. As we ate a focaccia baked in the sand, a sort of mouse appeared, erect as a kangaroo, with a tail that ended in a dainty tuft. It showed no fear: almost no one ever passes through here. It ate out of my hand. I was immediately overcome by the welfare syndrome that afflicts the white man in Africa: in addition to crumbs, I gave it water to drink in a canteen cap. Then we went to sleep. During the night, our beds under the stars were invaded by the jerboa (the scientific name for the wretched creature) and millions of his companions. Someone let out a yell: they were chewing on his ears. To his misfortune, he was sleeping right on the cloth where we had eaten. "The finest restaurant for jumping mice in the whole Sahara," the jerboa must have told his friends. I don't know what a jerboa weighs, but all together they created a furry, solid, snapping, all-encompassing mass. We abandoned the place. Months later, we returned to Laouni. We stopped to make camp. In the firelight, a little mouselike creature appeared (we all swore it was the same one as before). We immediately threw a shoe at him. He didn't come back, and that night we slept the peace of the just.

The harshness of the desert does not make it a simple place. The Sahara is a complex system whose highly sensitive variables and operators fluctuate as conditions change. A few grains of sand sliding down a dune can raise a storm with the help of the harmattan, the wind that drives men mad. The Tuareg, the desert's best-adapted inhabitants, are well aware that the Sahara is as complex and changing as a living organism. To them, the "desert of all deserts" is a giant who has been thrown to the ground by some unknown misfortune. He has been there for millions of years, on his back. His head is in the south, with his hair created by the rain forests of black Africa. His feet, stretching out to the north, are the peaks of the Moroccan Atlas Mountains. The giant has internal organs: sometimes humors are released, unexpected water or oil. Men collect his precious secretions: salt and surface minerals. His naked, smooth belly is the central desert, where dunes alternate with oases, like the pores of the skin.

Sometimes the titan moves, creating volcanoes like the Tibesti and mountains like the Hoggar. He has biological cycles that cause wind and palpitating sand, the heat of the rocks, and dew gathering in the caves. "Sometimes the skin on his chest flakes, when he sweats," an old man told me, indicating the abomination of eroded rocks around us. "That's the *hammada.*"

The men who wander this anthropomorphic territory, nomads who may be herders, warriors, or merchants, guarantee the flow and exchange of life. The Arabs, who take their name from the word *ar-rabiah* (the spring, when the dromedaries give birth and there is an abundance of milk, paradise on earth for a nomad), call the desert *al-badia,* which gave rise to the word *Bedouin.* But the word does not mean "abandoned place." It is a complex notion that has more of an ecological and anthropological meaning than a geographical or geological one: it is the environment on which the nomad bases his survival. *Al-badia* is the entire system: men, animals, resources, time frames, and customs that distinguish life. Ask a Bedouin or a Tuareg where his house is, where his relatives live, where he feels right with the world. He'll tell you "Fil-badia," "in the desert." But he certainly doesn't mean the empty space that the word *desert* evokes in our minds; this he calls *khala,* "the silent, lifeless place." And as we have seen, such a place is rare in the Sahara.

The Sahara system can be described scientifically and then perceived in human terms. Desert experts see the integration of three principal components: the territory (which defines a "where" and "how"), the people who inhabit it (the "who"), and the evolving history of the Sahara system (the "when"). Knowledge of the landscape and environment, from geography to climate, flora

to fauna, must be integrated with environmental changes and the history of the population (from prehistoric times to the ethnographic nomadism of yesterday) in order to shed light on a way, perhaps the only way, to live in the desert. In this sense, the book you have opened provides the most complete background possible for the scientific understanding of the Sahara.

"One does not live in the desert. One crosses it." So say the Bedouin, citing the survival strategy of perpetual movement. Others hole up in oases, artificial spaces created by hydric anomalies. In this back-and-forth movement from one end to the other, Sahara peoples construct their own perception of the environment. They see an invisible metropolis where space and time are virtual, yet perfectly identifiable through signs that are imperceptible to us. This self-knowledge of the Sahara can only be experienced, not learned.

In one of the incongruous lodges that provide a cup of green tea to the wayfarer, in the middle of nowhere across the longest roads through the Sahara, I met an "operator." He was a former philosophy student at the University of Algiers. "I got fed up and I started to sell tea to truck drivers. I add the leaves, they add the water," he told me. Using two hands, crouching on the ground, he gathered a big pile of sand before him. "This is a pile of sand," the philosopher said. "Yes," I agreed. Then he took a couple of grains of sand and threw them to the side. "Is it still a pile of sand?" he asked with the gentle smile of the Berbers. "Yes." He repeated the operation a number of times, almost dancing with his hands. Then he asked me: "With which grain of sand does the pile stop being a pile?" Where the Sahara begins and ends is not for men to know.

THE DISCOVERY OF THE SAHARA

THE HORSE PERIOD

20 FROM LEFT TO RIGHT SIXTEENTH-CENTURY PORTUGUESE MAP; SAHARAN OASES; YOUNG ALGERIAN MEN IN THE LATE 1800s; CITROËN EXPEDITION, 1922–1923.

21 ONLY THE PHYSICAL ENDURANCE OF THE DROMEDARY MADE IT POSSIBLE TO CROSS THE SAHARA.

22 A PYGMY STRUGGLES WITH A STORK IN A MOSAIC AT VILLA SILIA, LIBYA. EVEN IN CLASSICAL TIMES IT WAS KNOWN THAT A TRIBE OF "LITTLE MEN" LIVED BEYOND THE GREAT DESERT.

23 TOP BATTLES BETWEEN PYGMIES AND THE MOST FEROCIOUS, GIGANTIC AFRICAN ANIMALS ARE RECURRING THEMES IN ROMAN ARTWORK, AS SEEN IN THIS LIVELY PAINTING DISCOVERED IN THE PHYSICIAN'S HOUSE IN POMPEII.

23 BOTTOM HERODOTUS' STORIES OF THE GARAMANTES AND THEIR SWIFT CHARIOTS HAVE BEEN CONFIRMED BY THE DISCOVERY OF NUMEROUS GRAFFITI IN VARIOUS AREAS OF THE SAHARA. THE ENGRAVING SHOWN IS FOUND IN WADI DJERAT IN TASSILI N'AJJER.

Over the millennia, the Sahara has slowly shifted from fertile land to savanna, steppe, and finally desert in a gradual yet inexorable process of desertification that continues to this day. According to the first written sources we have, from ancient classical times, the Sahara was already an immense expanse of more or less terrible desolation that divided the territories of Mediterranean Africa from mysterious southern lands inhabited by peoples whose skins were blackened by the sun. But it was still nothing like it is today. The true desert begins much farther south now, and Libya, the name used by the Greeks to designate the whole stretch of North Africa, from Egypt to the Atlantic, is described in the *Odyssey* as an opulent land of animal breeders, "where prince or shepherd, all men have what they need, cheese, meat and fresh milk; the beasts are milked every day because the sheep give birth three times a year. . . ." These Libyans, ancestors of the Berbers, founded flourishing realms.

Writing in the fifth century B.C., Herodotus speaks of the Garamantes, perhaps the progenitors of the present-day Tuareg, who at that time had settled in Fezzan: "They chase the Ethiopian cave-dwellers on chariots drawn by four horses. This is because the Ethiopian cave-dwellers are faster runners than any men of whom we have ever heard speak." This brief comment contains two precious pieces of information: first, if we assume the existence of herds of horses, the desert must have had many more pastures and much more water than it does today, and second, even its northern area was inhabited by black-skinned peoples (to the Greeks, Ethiopians were all black-skinned Africans) who lived in the mountain caves. It is believed that their descendants are the Tebu of Tibesti. Herodotus also recounts the first crossing of the Sahara known to us, carried out by a group of young Nasamons, another Berber population that lived in Cyrenaica.

It appears that on a bet, these bold young men went fearlessly into the desolation of the south, and after passing through "a region of ferocious beasts" and walking for days and days in the sand (luckily they had supplied themselves with water and food), they finally arrived in a region full of trees and pastures. "There," the Greek historian states, "they were attacked by some small men shorter than the average, who seized them and carried them away. The language of these dwarves was incomprehensible, and for their part, they could not understand the Nasamons. They carried the prisoners over a vast stretch of swampy land and then arrived in a city where the inhabitants were all black and just as small. A large, crocodile-infested river flowed next to the city from west to east." Perhaps it was the Niger, on whose shores Pygmy tribes lived at that time.

25 **LEFT** Discovered in a Roman villa in Tunisia and exhibited at the Bardo Museum in Tunis, this mosaic provides a faithful rendering of an African elephant. Precious elephant tusks reached Mediterranean ports across the Sahara on long lines of horse-drawn wagons.

25 **RIGHT** Surrounded by wild beasts, Africa vaunts its riches, including the inevitable ivory. This lunette at the Villa del Casale was probably the work of North African artisans.

24–25 The mosaic of the hunting party in the Villa del Casale at Piazza Armerina, Sicily, shows the boarding of exotic animals captured in North Africa. Such animals were in great demand for the circus games of imperial Rome.

Apart from "explorations" of this nature, what we know for certain is that in classical times, the Phoenician and Greek cities that sprang up on the North African coast—Carthage, Sabratha, Oea, Leptis Magna, and Cyrene—were Mediterranean terminuses along a lucrative trans-Sahara trade route that supplied highly prized products to Europe from "black" Africa: ostrich feathers, ivory, slaves, and huge amounts of gold. Traffic was handled by native peoples, the Garamantes in particular; very rarely did Greek or Phoenician coastal traders join the caravans. We know that one of them, the Carthaginian Magone, crossed the desert three times, an enterprise that was considered highly exceptional.

These goods, which also included ebony, wild animals for circus spectacles, and precious stones known as "garamantines," arrived in more copious amounts when the Romans, having destroyed their rival Carthage and conquered North Africa all the way to Morocco, diverted goods from all over the world, especially luxury items, to omnivorous Rome. Interest in desert trade routes, at that time traveled by long processions of horse-drawn carts, was so strong that Rome decided to assume direct control and organize conquering expeditions. In 19 B.C., the consul Cornelius Balbo left from Sabratha and marched to Phazania (today's Fezzàn) with an army of fifteen or twenty thousand men. This implies that numerous abundant wells must have existed to slake the thirst of so many people along a route nearly 435 miles long. A century later, under the emperor Domitian, historical sources unfortunately speak only briefly of three expeditions that must have pushed far beyond Fezzàn, all the way to a "great river" that once again could have been the Niger. But these were sporadic initiatives that had no long-lasting consequences, and although the generals returning to Rome celebrated impressive triumphs, trade remained firmly in the hands of desert peoples. And once the Roman Empire's power waned, they no longer grew rich from commerce, but through devastating raids on Romanized territories.

26 Squealing trumpets and drum rolls celebrate the arrival of a caravan, reaching its destination after an often excruciating, dangerous crossing.

27 In the so-called Cantino Map (1501–1505), the Sahara is almost nonexistent, crushed between the mass of the Montes Claros (Atlas Mountains) to the north and the legendary Castello da Mina, a Portuguese settlement on the coast of Guinea to the south.

During this period a fundamental innovation occurred that would keep the increasingly arid Sahara in its role of commercial bridge between the Mediterranean and the Sudan: the introduction of the dromedary, the camel with one hump that was probably brought from Asia to North Africa between the third and fourth centuries A.D. A humble, simple animal, the dromedary can go for days and days without drinking and can nourish itself on thorny bushes. It was a "desert ship" that enabled wanderers to travel from oasis to oasis, those islands of life in an ocean of desolation. For centuries, it allowed nomads to cross the increasingly arid expanse of sand and rocks, which had become too hostile for horses. Thanks to the caravans of camels, with their light saddles and the leather sheepskin waterbags they carried, it was possible to travel increasingly lengthy distances between the scattered wells. And when the Arabs invaded North Africa, the camel made it possible to found fabulous flourishing cities on the two shores of the solid sea known as the Sahara. These cities included Sigilmassa, on the Moroccan threshold of the Sahara, with its stone walls and profusion of palaces surrounded by villas and gardens, where the caravans loaded up the gold of Belèd-es-Sudàn, the "Land of the Blacks," and returned south loaded with red copper, wool clothing, turbans, drugs, perfumes, and dates. Another city was Audagost, where the women excelled in preparing nut cakes, macaroni with honey, camel with truffles, and serpent with wormwood. And Ghana, one of the southern terminuses, the capital of a large African empire whose king had horses decked with gold and mastiffs that wore silver collars. And Mali, which in the fourteenth century became the richest city in the Sudan and whose king owned "a virgin gold stone that has never seen fire, so heavy that twenty men can barely move it, and to which he ties his horse."

The first tale of a desert crossing that has survived to our time comes from this fortunate period. It was accomplished by someone

who is considered the greatest of all Arab travelers: Muhammed ibn Abdallah al-Lavati, better known as Ibn Battutah (which means "Son of the Duck"). Born in Tangiers in 1304, Ibn Battutah left his family and homeland at age twenty-one to make a pilgrimage to Mecca, and ended up traveling his whole life. He visited the vast Islamic Orient and went by sea to India, China, and East Africa. In 1352, he followed the Sigilmassa-Mali route, joining a caravan of traders. He saw houses made of salt bricks and roofs of camel hide. He saw miserable villages where pounds of gold dust were exchanged. He saw the desert of sand that was "luminous and shining, that expands the chest and gives a feeling of euphoria." He passed through swarms of flies and hordes of lice, which did not bite him because he wore a flacon of mercury around his neck. He went unharmed past the demons that infested the dunes and enchanted travelers, making them lose their way and die of thirst. He suffered hunger and thirst, and when he arrived in the Land of the Blacks, he found them ill-mannered and shameless, as women were held in higher esteem than men, and he was disappointed by their hospitality, because at the welcoming feast there was nothing more than half a gourd of ground millet with a bit of honey and milk. And he was even more dissatisfied with the farewell gift he received from the king of Mali: three loaves of bread and a piece of fried beef.

He took a different road back, this time crossing lands infested with deadly scorpions and the territory of the Hoggar Tuareg, "veiled people who bode no good." But he was lucky, because it was the month of Ramadan, when those marauders temporarily ceased their predations. It was late 1353 when he saw Sigilmassa once again. With all the author's idiosyncrasies, his report gives the Sahara a largely positive image: a land where life is hard but not impossible, except in a few particular areas, where a certain prosperity was possible because of trade and well-organized caravans.

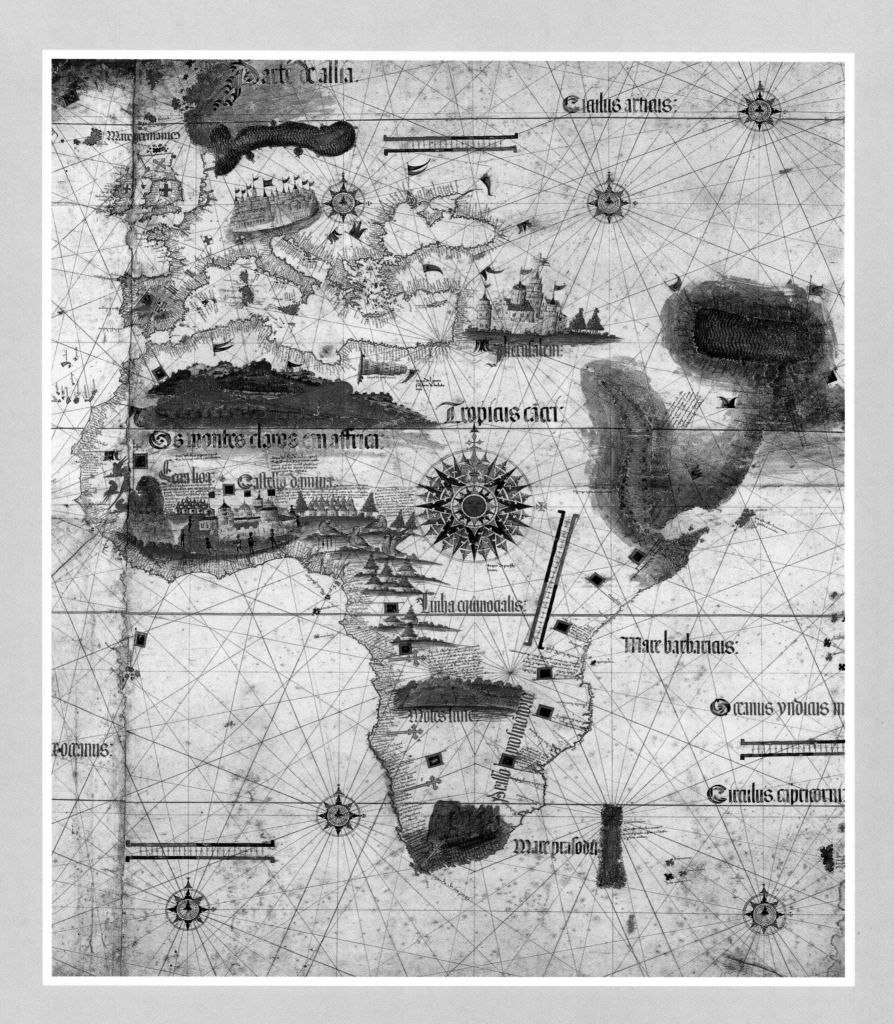

Jetrain

Questi sono pa
ludi gradissi
mi de iql nasce
questo fiume e ck
chia

manilo

paludæ

chucuben

palude

isola

chucho garāga

chon

daxo

lago

angalā

çalon

piade

organa

chidin

mons pollaza

Io ho notado te sopra
chel nilo nasce i abassia traco
prouicie.zoe marora ouer meroa.
e salgu ma jlibri punici dicono ch
nasce imauritania. laqual cossa
io nõ credo tuta esser uera chel nil
habi qui el origine ple informatiõ
ho habuto ma che questo sia uno ramo
vel nilo io affermo. pche se truoua qli
simili   animali che se truoua nel
nilo.

Stach

P. lidi

bolala

agran

bargemi

lago

Hain.

mandera

sengi primi

bolaglia
garimander

tombact

ME RGI

patati

mergi

cusha

non

rigabelao

ORGANA

engeco

calen

calen

deserto

AFRICA

Ff che sono molti cosmograp hi e dottissimi
homeni iqual scruieño che in ãsta affrice. ma
xime nele mauritanie esseruj molti mõstruo
si homeni e aiali. pino necessario qnotar el parer mio. nõ
pho che io uogli ptradir ale autorita de tati ma pdir la diligētia ho
habuta i inqrir tute le nouita sea possuto iuestigā p molti anni de
ãsta affrica começato dalibia barbaria etute le mauritanie pfina al
fiume valoro a da 17 mõti a tuerso p era de neg oltra el pmo clima e de
soto começato dbiminuagra marocho. fessa. sigil mesa e p quela costiera

DESERTO

curbi

durzo

THE QUEEN OF SAHARA

Along with the goods of Belèd-es-Sudàn, exaggerated reports of the wealth across the Sahara reached as far as Europe. It quickly spurred aspiring Marco Polos from Genoa, Provence, and Catalonia to depart for those tantalizing destinations. They would conclude excellent business deals but remain unknown until the last century, because unlike Marco Polo, they did not write renowned accounts of their African adventures, and their letters remained buried in archives. For example, there was an anonymous merchant from Genoa who came to Sigilmassa around 1300 and became the first European to hear about the Tuareg, "who always go about with their mouths covered." And Anselmo d'Ysalguier of Toulouse crossed the desert, reached Gao in 1410, fell in love with a native princess and brought her home with a dowry of gold dust and precious stones. Another Genovese, Antonio Malfante, visited Tuat in 1447 and was quite impressed with both the wealth of the Jewish merchants—in terms of business, some historians call the Middle Ages "the Jewish era of the Sahara"—and, most importantly, with the veiled Tuareg, who claim they are the descendants of the biblical Philistines. But Malfante was unable to discover where all their gold came from, because, of course, the people he asked were not that ingenuous, and he returned home singing the praises of vegetable butter, which he considered "marvelous." A quarter of a century later, a Florentine named Benedetto Dei wandered the Sahara, getting as far as a certain Tambettu, which may be Timbuktu, where he did "a fair amount of business" and where "bolts of cloth and herringbone wool and ghurnelli cloth with that ribbing they make in Lombardy" were sold.

During this same period, Portuguese ships were making their way farther and farther south along the coast of Africa: to the west, they established scattered footholds and trading posts. The most important of these, Elmina, was located in what at the time was called the Gold Coast and is now the coast of Ghana. In 1483, a sort of diplomatic-mercantile legation left here heading for Timbuktu, which in the European imagination was already becoming legendary as the Queen of the Desert. The idea was to divert trans-Sahara traffic to the Gulf of Guinea, replacing the caravans with ships. This would have cut off the North African Islamic states and dealt a mortal blow to those enemies of Christianity. We do not know exactly how things went, but of eight hopefuls sent, only one returned, and even he came back in bad shape.

The legend of Timbuktu as a sort of African Eldorado persisted until late in the nineteenth century. It was consecrated in *Africa Descriptio,* a great treatise on the geography of the dark continent written by a man who had personally visited many of the locations he mentions: Alhassan ibn Mohammed Alwazzan. Born in Granada in Andalusia around 1493, he emigrated with his family to Morocco to flee the forced conversion to Christianity imposed by the Spanish sovereigns. After traveling throughout the Maghreb and the Near East, Alwazzan was captured by Sicilian corsairs in the water off Tripoli and given to Pope Leo X as a slave who could be useful due to his vast knowledge. In 1520 he converted, perhaps in order to get out of Castel Sant'Angelo, where he had been locked up for a year, and took the name Leo Africanus, which he used as a pen name for his work, written in Italian. His writings were published in Venice in 1550 by Ramusio in his great collection *Delle navigazioni e viaggi.* Geographers and cartographers used it as a reference for three whole centuries. Between 1509 and 1513, Leo Africanus crossed the Sahara in all directions, from north to south, east to west, Morocco to the Niger, and the Niger to the Nile. His description of Timbuktu, where he often stayed for long periods, reveals an opulent mercantile capital:

"It is about 12 miles from a branch of the Niger, and its houses are huts made of poles, covered with clay, with straw roofs. There is a temple of stone and mortar, made by a fine master from Granada, and similarly, a great palace made by the same artisan, where the king resides. And in this city there are many workshops of artisans and merchants, mostly weavers of cotton wool cloth; this city receives European cloths brought by merchants from Barbary. The women of this city still cover their faces, except for the female slaves, who sell everything one eats; and the inhabitants are very rich people, especially the foreigners who often live here, and the present king has even given his two daughters in marriage to two merchant brothers, so moved was he by their wealth. In this city there are also many fresh water wells, although when the Niger rises, it flows into certain canals near the city. . . . There is a great abundance of grain and animals, as they are quite fond of milk and butter; but there is very little salt, so that it is brought from Tegaza, which is about five hundred miles from Timbuktu.

"The king owns great wealth in gold piastre and bullion, some of which weigh one thousand three hundred pounds. His court is quite orderly and magnificent, and when he goes from one city to another with his courtiers, he rides on a camel and his servants lead the horses by hand; and if he goes to battle, they tie the camels and all soldiers ride on horseback. Whenever one wants to speak to this king, one must kneel before him, and take a handful of earth and sprinkle it on one's head and shoulders: and this is the obeisance that one makes, but only by those who have not spoken further with him, or by ambassadors. He keeps about three thousand horses, and an infinite number of footmen, who carry bows made of wild fennel sticks, which they use to shoot poisoned arrows. They often make war against nearby ene-

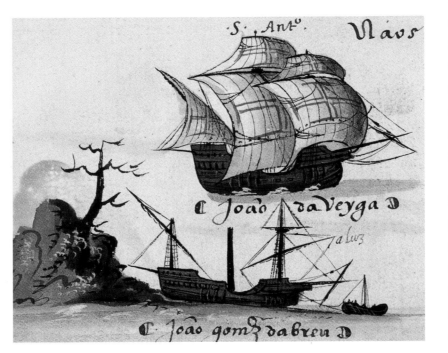

mies and those to whom they desire to give no tribute, and when they win, in Timbuktu they sell the youths taken in battle.

"No horses are born in this land, except for a few fine small mounts that merchants also use for their travels, and a few courtiers in the city. But the good horses come from Barbary. The king sends for a number of them, and twelve are sent, and he immediately selects the one he prefers and pays for it quite honestly.

"This king is a great enemy of the Jews and wants none of them to stay within his city. There are many judges, doctors and priests in the city, all paid well by the king, and the king greatly honors literary men. There are also many hand-written books for sale that come

from Barbary, and there is more profit in this than in any of the other goods. In place of money, they use pieces of pure, unadulterated gold, and for small things little shells from Persia, worth four hundred to a ducat. Usually these inhabitants are good-natured men, and they have the custom of wandering about after ten o'clock at night until one o'clock in the morning, playing music and dancing throughout the city, and the citizens keep many male and female slaves for their needs. This city is quite susceptible to the dangers of fire, and during my second voyage here, almost half the city burned within the space of five hours. Around it are no gardens or any fruitful place."

Leo Africanus also speaks of the routes followed by desert caravans across "harsh and dolorous" lonely places where "due to the great heat and lack of water, many men and animals die," and described the various peoples that he encountered at the oases, including the Tuareg:

"Those who have not seen them could not believe the patience with which they suffer hunger. They do not have the custom of eating bread or food of any kind, but they are nourished by the milk of their camels, and their custom is to drink a great ladle of that milk in the morning, warm from the camels. In the evening, they eat a certain dry meat, boiled in milk and butter. When it is cooked, they each seize their portion in their hands, and when they have eaten, they drink that broth, using their hands instead of a spoon. Then they drink a cup of milk, and this is the end of the supper. They live without rules or reason. The gentlemen of this people wear a black cloth on their head and use a part of it to cover the face, hiding everything except the eyes. And they wear this always, so that, when they want to eat, each time they put the food in their mouth they uncover the mouth, and when they have eaten they cover it once again. They say that the reason for this custom is that since it is shameful for man to expel

31 LEFT KING SEBASTIAN OF PORTUGAL LOST HIS LIFE IN THE BATTLE OF ALCAZAR-QUIVIR, WHERE THE MOROCCAN TROOPS OF AL-MANSUR EMERGED VICTORIOUS.

31 RIGHT THE TUAREG, TRUE LORDS OF THE DESERT, LIVED BY RAIDING RICH CARAVANS OR EXACTING TOLLS FROM ANYONE WHO CROSSED THEIR TERRITORY.

food, so is it shameful to ingest it. Their women are quite small and fleshy, but not very white. Their behinds are quite full and fat, as are their breasts and bosom; their waists are quite narrow. They are pleasing women both in mind and touch of hand, and sometimes they will allow themselves to be kissed, but it is dangerous to go further, because one may be ruthlessly killed for such a reason. These peoples are also quite independent, as these lands make it too vexatious to go to their pavilions, and they do not frequent the main roads. But the caravans that cross their deserts must pay their princes a certain tax, which for each camel load equals a cloth equal to the value of one ducat." At that time, Timbuktu and the entire south-central area of the western Sahara, with the extremely important salt mines of Tegaza, belonged to the African empire of the Songhai, whose capital was Gao, on the Niger. Its greatest king, Askia Mohammed, reigned from 1493 to 1529. Yet its very prosperity caused the downfall of that magnificent state. Under sultan al-Mansur, Morocco yearned after Sudanese gold. In 1583, the sultan sent a legation to Gao whose secret mission was to reconnoiter the place and assess the military power of the Songhai. The pomp with which the legation was received did nothing but further inflame Moroccan greed. The sultan promptly sent an army of twenty thousand men across the desert. Decimated by thirst and hunger, the survivors took Tegaza and its salt mines, but could go no further: in the Sahara, it was impossible to find supplies for such a large army. Al-Mansur saw this and changed tactics. In late 1590, the enterprise was handled by an expedition of a few hundred men. This elite force was equipped with the most recent firearms, which the Songhai were desperately lacking. Almost all of these musketeers, harquebusiers, and artillerymen were renegade Spanish, Portuguese, and Italian Christians that the Moroccans called Rumì. After the trials of the desert, these conquistadors at the service of Islam celebrated their

arrival at the fresh waters of the Niger with an orgiastic feast, then they confronted the forty thousand warriors of the Songhai army and routed them. Gao and Timbuktu fell. Endless lines of camels arrived in Marrakech, all loaded with booty—gold dust, slaves, musk, ebony, and all the wealth of Belèd-es-Sudàn, which never recovered from the disaster. At the gate of the sultan's palace, fourteen thousand goldsmiths worked day after day on the conquered gold. Like his counterpart in the imaginary El Dorado the Spaniards sought in America, Al-Mansur took the title of el-Dehebi, the Golden One. The entire western Sahara was now part of the Moroccan empire, but its trade was ruined. The collapse of the Songhai resulted in anarchy, and the territory fragmented into a mosaic of fragile states. Tribes robbed caravans, and gold took other, safer routes toward Tunis, Tripoli, and European trading posts on the coast of Guinea. Timbuktu, governed first by a Moroccan pasha and then by the descendants of the Rumì, remained the Queen of the Sahara only in the imaginations of countless seekers of legendary realms. The news of the rich treasure the sultan of Morocco had amassed spurred companies of English and French adventurers to attempt to reach the fabulous city, only to have their ships run aground just a few short miles down the course of the Gambia or the Senegal, which in murky seventeenth-century African geography fought for the honor of being the mouth of the Niger.

During the Age of Enlightenment, the lust for riches was replaced by the yearning for knowledge. In addition to that unattainable Timbuktu, there was another mystery to explore—the existence of an immense inland sea in the Sahara that later proved to be muddy, miasmatic Lake Chad. In 1788, a group of eminent persons from the British scientific, financial, and political world founded the Association for Promoting the Discovery of the Interior of Parts of Africa, whose name clearly reveals its program. It immediately organized discovery missions. The sailor John Ledyard departed that same year with the ambitious goal of crossing straight across thousands of miles of desert, from the Nile to the Atlantic. He died of fever in Cairo while he was still organizing his caravan. Also in 1788, William Lucas, former English vice consul in Morocco, headed to Tripoli, from which he was to travel south until he came out in the Gulf of Guinea. He never even left the Mediterranean, getting no farther than Misurata. Major Houghton met a worse fate. He chose a western itinerary, but was assassinated on the threshold of the Mauri Sahara. In 1795, the young Scottish surgeon Mungo Park offered the African

Association his services, which were accepted. His task was to follow the course of the enigmatic Niger and visit Timbuktu. He drowned in that river during his second voyage in 1805 while under attack by hostile natives. Just a few days earlier, he had reached the river port of the legendary city but had been prevented from docking there.

A similar fate was in store for the German Friedrich Hornemann, a theology student. Twenty-five years old with an athletic build, he was an expert in the natural sciences and meteorology and spoke Arabic well. The Association felt he was an ideal candidate, and in 1797 sent him to Egypt, from where he was to proceed to the Sahara. The French landing complicated matters, but in the end even Bonaparte gave his blessings to the enterprise. Along with another German, Josef Freudenberg, who had converted to Islam, Hornemann was able to met up with a caravan of pilgrims returning to Fezzan after a pilgrimage to Mecca.

Masquerading under the name Yussuf, Hornemann pretended to be a Mamluk. At the Siwa oasis he saw the imposing remains of the temple of Jupiter Ammon, where Alexander the Great had proclaimed himself the son of a god, and he saw innumerable caves full of mummies at the Mount of Embalmed Bodies. He was greeted by the squeal of trumpets at the Augila oasis, while his escort rode behind the green banner of the Prophet. Barefoot as a sign of respect, he kissed the hand of the sultan of Murzuch, the capital of Fezzan, who greeted him throned on an ancient ivory chair. But Freudenberg died here of fever, and Hornemann returned to Tripoli, to depart once again for the south in December 1799. He passed Fezzan, crossed the desert, reached Bornu, and from there went west, toward the great Niger River, which he reached in the summer of 1800, only to die of dysentery near the same place where Mungo Park would die five years later. The itinerary that Hornemann followed nevertheless seems the most feasible. After a long hiatus caused by the Napoleonic wars, explorations started up again from Tripoli. By order of the Ottoman government, its Turkish pasha collaborated and in March 1819 willingly allowed the scientist Joseph Ritchie and Captain George Francis Lyon of the Royal Navy to join a caravan heading to Murzuch. It was a hard voyage, with continuous sandstorms caused by the *simùn,* the terrible desert wind, which charged the atmosphere with electricity and caused sparks to fly from the horses' tails. Still, the company was pleasant and deferential, as the camel drivers had somehow come to believe that Ritchie was the son-in-law of the king of England. With his compass and astrolabe, Lyon himself passed for a necromancer; as the desert navigators knew that ships wandered in eternal darkness, broken only by their great lanterns, in that sea with no sun or moon, they had great esteem for the Atlantic sailor. But once he arrived in Murzuch, Ritchie sickened and died, and instead of proceeding toward Bornu, Lyon was forced to turn back, after witnessing the festive arrival of a caravan of slaves captured by the Tuareg, "the most beautiful race of men ever seen."

34–35 A WELL, A CIRCLE OF VEGETATION, AND A FEW PALMS: THIS IS A TYPICAL SAHARA OASIS, A LONG-AWAITED SOURCE OF SURVIVAL IN THE IMMENSE EXPANSE OF DUNES. THIS ILLUSTRATION COMES FROM THE TRAVEL DIARY OF THE ENGLISHMEN CENHAM, CLAPPERTON, AND OUDNEY.

35 LEFT In 1822, the Scotsman Hugh Clapperton joined Oudney's expedition and reached Lake Chad after crossing the Sahara. In 1825, after his return, he began a new exploratory trip and traveled from the Gulf of Guinea up to Sokoto, Nigeria, where he died in 1827.

35 RIGHT Dixon Denham joined Clapperton and Hillman on Oudney's expedition. He explored the lands south of Lake Chad, forming a warm friendship with the local sultan.

THE FIRST EXPLORATIONS

In 1822, the people of Murzuch, now accustomed to visits from curious strangers, greeted four other Englishmen: Clapperton, Hillman, Oudney, and Denham. *"Ingliz, ingliz!"* they cheered when the group arrived at the Fezzan oasis. After overcoming a few difficulties, the quartet succeeded in proceeding with a large group of Arab merchants following the "bone road," the caravan route marked by whitening skeletons of countless slaves who had died of privation along the way. They were the first Europeans to meet the Tebu of the Tibesti, who were poor, peaceful, filthy, and cheerful. In Bilma, a main stopover, the women met each caravan with elegant dances accompanied by the music of a goatskin-covered gourd. Beyond Bilma there were ten endless days of hellish desert. But then, crossing the borders of Bornu, they saw something in the distance that at first seemed nothing more than a mirage. It was actually the endless expanse of the waters of Lake Chad,

with dense reeds and acacias on its banks, populated by gigantic elephants, monstrous buffaloes, hippopotamuses, crocodiles, antelopes, and thousands of gazelles that ran among the thickets of tamarinds and carob trees. It was a Garden of Eden after weeks of limy sand and scorching rocks. The black sultanates of that region of Africa, Bornu, Baghirmi, Uadai, and Haussa, reminded the English of Arthurian knights covered in chain mail, with lancers protected by padded doublets, flag-bearers who unfurled long standards of red silk with verses from the Koran, sovereigns granting audiences from their thrones to the sound of trumpets, courtiers made even more plump by artificial bellies, and banquets with seventy different dishes served. Unfortunately, the climate was deadly, and Oudney fell victim to it. The survivors took off for the desert again in August 1824 and returned to Tripoli in January of the following year.

36 THE FIRST WHITE MAN TO REACH THE LEGENDARY TIMBUKTU AND LIVE TO TELL THE TALE WAS THE FRENCHMAN RENÉ CAILLÉ, SHOWN HERE (RIGHT) IN A SCENE AS IMAGINARY AS THE VIEW OF THE CITY (LEFT). IN REALITY, HE DISGUISED HIMSELF AS AN ARAB AND HAD TO BE EXTREMELY CAREFUL NOT TO REVEAL THAT HE WAS A EUROPEAN.

37 TOP IN GREAT DECLINE SINCE ITS GOLDEN DAYS, TIMBUKTU WAS AN ENORMOUS DISAPPOINTMENT FOR CAILLÉ, WHO SAW ONLY THE MISERABLE REMAINS OF ITS LOST GRANDEUR.

37 BOTTOM AS HE WANDERED THROUGH TIMBUKTU DRESSED AS AN EGYPTIAN REFUGEE, CAILLÉ HAD TIME TO DO BAS-RELIEFS OF THE CITY'S MAIN BUILDINGS, SUCH AS THIS MOSQUE.

During that period, someone finally managed to enter the impenetrable Timbuktu. Major Alexander Gordon Laing also departed from Tripoli to diagonally traverse the Sahara, going through Gadàmes, In Salah, and Tanezruft. He was favored by the Azger Tuareg, and their sheik accompanied him for a time, but Hoggar rivals attacked and gravely wounded him. Aided by several Mauri, Laing recovered and was able to enter the city of his dreams on August 18, 1826. He was driven out a month later, although in the beginning his presence was peaceably tolerated. On his way across the desert he was strangled by his guide. The first European to see Timbuktu and survive was the Frenchman René Caillé. Lured by a prize offered by the Geographic Society of Paris, and even more by the thrill of adventure, this twenty-eight-year-old, the modest, intelligent son of a poor provincial baker who had died in misery, learned a bit of Arabic and received instruction on Islam. He then masqueraded as an Egyptian brought to France by Napoleon's soldiers while still a child, forcefully converted but still a Muslim in his heart, and desirous of returning to his land and family. Dressed as an Arab, traveling under the name of Abdallahi, and demonstrating all the necessary devotion, in March 1827, he left Sierra Leone with the declared goal of going to Timbuktu, to there join a caravan that would take him to Egypt. Hardship and illness did not stop him, and the heart-wrenching story he told at each stop was believed. After a year of punishing marches, he entered the great city of Djenné on the Niger, a rich

trading center of over ten thousand inhabitants, and here he embarked on a large dugout loaded with goods and slaves. He disembarked on April 20, 1828, at the river port of Cabra. From there to Timbuktu by foot would take just a few hours. He entered the following day, on horseback, in the company of a slave trader. His disappointment has become famous in the annals of explorations. What he found were rambling shacks, a mass of beggars, a miserable market, a total of eight mosques, whitish sand in every direction, a dreadful silence (because without trees there were no birds), and malodorous smoke (because without wood the only fuel was camel dung). "All the encroaching sleepiness, inertia, and sadness of the deserts" seemed to have bewitched the decaying Queen of the Sahara, which only a century before had boasted one hundred thousand inhabitants; it was now reduced to a tenth of that. After a two-week stay, Caillé decided he had had enough, and he joined a six-hundred-camel caravan heading to Morocco. This was the worst part of his adventure. During the summer months, the wells were almost dry, and the already harsh route became excruciatingly difficult. What was more, his traveling companions did not treat the supposed Abdallahi very well, perhaps because they were suspicious of him. He was mistreated, humiliated, and slapped around like a slave. In Arauan, at the southern edge of the desert, they pointed out the bones of the hapless Gordon Laing, left to the crows. Perhaps it was a taunting admonition. No matter, his odyssey had came to an end. On August 12, Caillé arrived in Fez and on September 7 in Tangiers, where, ragged and covered in sores, he came before the astounded commander of the French naval station. He received his promised prize but was unable to enjoy for very long. Weakened by the hardships he had endured, he died in 1838, just forty years old. His final years were embittered by controversy: some accused him of deception, including using the notes left by Gordon Laing to make up his story.

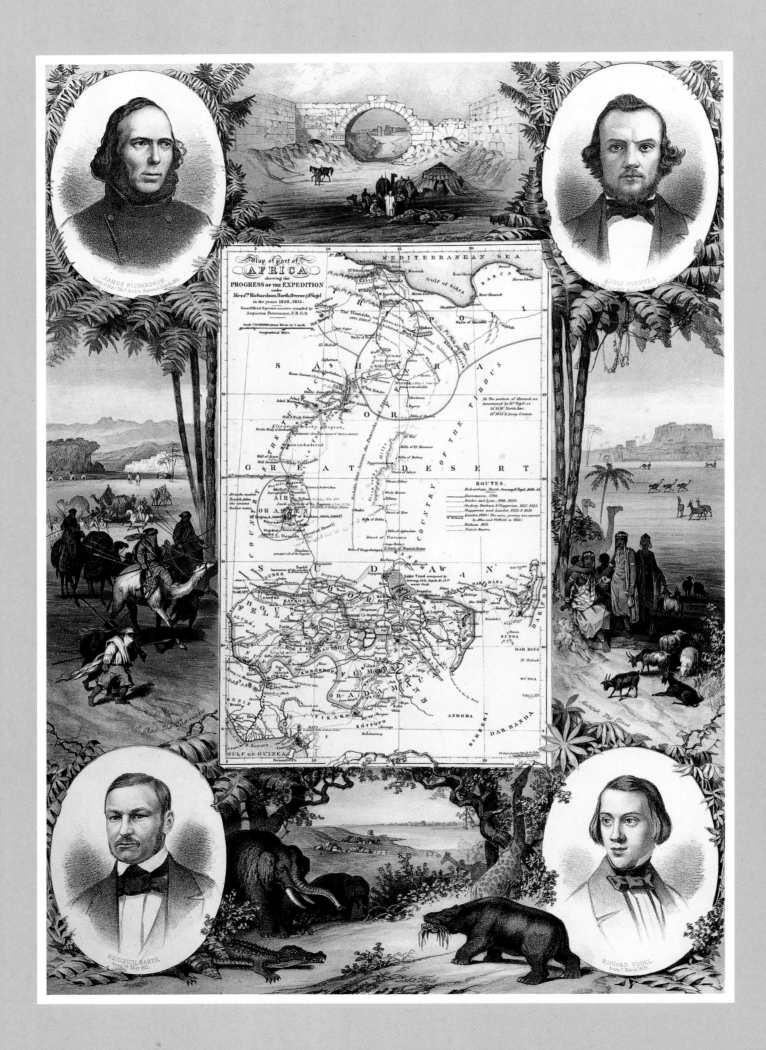

38 In 1850, the Englishman James Richardson led a great expedition from Tripoli with the Germans Adolf Overweg and Heinrich Barth. He got as far as Bornu, where he died of fever. Another German, Eduard Vogel, followed in his footsteps in 1853 and traveled all through Bornu, but was killed three years later. The four explorers (clockwise from top left) are pictured here around a map of Central Africa.

39 Twenty-five years after Caillé, the naturalist Heinrich Barth (left) mended a broken heart by setting out to explore Africa, where he also saw Timbuktu (right).

After reaching its most coveted destination, exploration in the Sahara seemed to need a pause. A good twenty years passed before the next great voyage. It was organized by the Englishman James Richardson for purposes that were not only scientific, but also commercial and humanitarian. The idea was to enter into a relationship with the Tuareg, supplying them with goods in exchange for their giving up the slave trade. Traveling with Richardson, who left from Tripoli in 1850, were two German naturalists, Adolf Overweg and Heinrich Barth (who willingly accepted that leap into the unknown as a way to get over a failed love affair).

Disguised as Arabs, fully armed in order to command respect, and accompanied by five servants and about twenty camels loaded with every kind of cargo imaginable, including a collapsible boat to navigate Lake Chad, the three traveled down to Fezzan and from there left for the Gat oasis, where negotiations to convince the Tuareg to join the antislavery faction were met with nothing but ironic smiles. The trio then headed south, touching the Hoggar Massif and crossing the mountains of Air, where another legendary Saharan city, Agàdez, awaited them. This was the final stop of the Tripoli caravan route, just as Timbuktu was the last stop for the Moroccan route, and like Timbuktu, it was impoverished and depopulated. Of its former fifty thousand inhabitants, only five or six thousand remained. Everywhere Barth noted "the vestiges of a vanished splendor . . . on the walls, which are falling into ruins, ravening vultures perch, waiting to seize some piece of refuse." Separated from Richardson, who died not far from there, struck down by a tropical disease, the two Germans traveled around the endless swamps of Chad, where Overweg also succumbed.

Left alone, Barth gave up his original plans to travel to the far-off coast of eastern Africa across from Zanzibar, and headed west, penetrating the vast, still unknown regions of the central Niger. In September 1853, he came to Timbuktu, which for some years had been in the hands of the Tuareg. He remained for six months, pretending to be an Arab. His situation was precarious and semi-clandestine, although he was protected by a sheik who prevented his fanatical countrymen from bringing Barth to the same end as Gordon Laing, whom some believed was Barth's father. He remained hidden, and the few times he went out he had to be surrounded by an armed Tuareg escort. But in that city that had been celebrated by the scholars of Islam for its wealth of libraries, he had the good fortune to discover a text that had seemed lost for good: the manuscript of Tarikh-es-Sudan, the history of the Songhai empire, written in 1640 by Ahmed Baba. With this precious booty he left for Gao, yet another decaying capital with crumbling mosques and clusters of rickety huts leaning against the ruins. In December 1854, Barth returned to Lake Chad in Kuka, where he was surprised to find a compatriot, the scientist Eduard Vogel, who was there to do research. In the fall of 1855, as Barth was crossing back over the Sahara toward Tripoli, Vogel entered the still unknown Uadai, where, in February 1856, he made the mistake of climbing a sacred mountain. His punishment was death. After returning to England in 1859, Barth published a complete account of his long adventure, *Travels and Discoveries in North and Central Africa,* five massive volumes that make up a sort of epic encyclopedia.

40 THE KHEDIVE OF EGYPT SUPPORTED ROHLFS' EXPEDITION THROUGH THE LIBYAN DESERT SO THAT HE MIGHT STUDY THE POSSIBILITY OF BRINGING NILE WATERS TO THE SAHARA OASES.

41 TOP GERHARD ROHLFS IS SHOWN HERE WITH HIS TWO TRAVELING COMPANIONS IN DAHKLA IN THE LIBYAN DESERT, WHICH THE EXPEDITION REACHED IN JANUARY 1874.

41 BOTTOM LEFT ROHLFS REACHED EGYPT'S KHARGA OASIS IN MARCH 1874.

41 BOTTOM RIGHT THE PHOTOGRAPHER FOR ROHLFS' EXPEDITION, PHILIPPE REMELÉ, TOOK THIS SHOT OF THE NEW MUSLIM NECROPOLIS IN ASYUT, EGYPT.

Reading these books and meeting the author inspired a young French aristocrat, the nineteen-year-old Henri Duveyrier. He was already enamored of the desert, whose northern edge he had skirted as an adolescent with his father, departing from Algiers. France, which occupied the Algerian coast in 1830, had been slowly pushing south for about twenty years, beyond the Atlas Mountains, and was organizing exploratory expeditions to the Saharan oases. After an initial incursion in 1859 to Mzab and El Golea, which had never been visited by a European, and from which he had fled, eating nothing but lizards along the way because the natives refused to give him food, in 1860, Duveyrier was appointed to an official mission that interested the emperor Napoleon III himself: exploring the Tunisian and Tripoline south to verify the importance of the trading routes. Duveyrier subsequently risked having his throat cut, being poisoned, being stoned, and dying of thirst, but managed to be received by the Azger Tuareg and gain the friendship of one of their sheiks, who had once helped Gor-

don Laing and had learned to count to ten in English. This "magnificent and majestic" old man helped Duveyrier enter the oasis of Gadàmes, a city surrounded by date palms and walls, with white houses crowded against each other to protect against the burning sun. Here, in the shade of the thickets, the Frenchman learned the language and script of the Tuareg, whose lifestyle he admired. "With weapons from which strips of variously decorated leather hang, with their fanciful clothing and their immobility on the imposing animal with its slow and regular pace, they have something that reminds me of the times of the knights in armor. And truly the Tuareg have something knightly that I like."

After once again risking his life to visit Gat, whose Arabic residents drove him out, and turning toward Fezzan, Duveyrier was unable to obtain permission to penetrate the Hoggar, and returned home with his body ruined by hardship. He was just twenty-one and his career as an explorer was already over. But as he was also a brilliantly gifted writer, his book, *Les Touaregs du Nord,* published in 1865 and a milestone in Saharan ethnography, created a new legend of the veiled paladins of the desert. The myth has survived almost completely intact down to our times, continuously revived by novels and films.

French Algeria was the starting point for another great explorer of the Sahara, the German Gerhard Rohlfs. After enlisting in the foreign legion, this restless young man decided to seek his fortune within the depths of the Dark Continent, perhaps in Timbuktu, whose fame had evidently not been wholly tarnished. In 1861, Rohlfs left for Tangiers and spent some time in Morocco, learning Arabic and pretending to be a Muslim, shaved and circumcised. A year later, he left for the Sahara, passing Wadi Draa and reaching the oasis of Tafilalet. However, he was suspected of espionage and was attacked by his guides, who left him for dead. He was rescued and cared for by two poor marabouts and managed to return to Algeria. He went back to his saviors in 1864 and with their assistance penetrated unknown Tuat. He could not travel to the Hoggar due to a war among the Tuareg, so he headed to Tripoli, going through Gadàmes. Then he headed out to the desert again, crossing Fezzan and reaching Bornu to follow the Benue River to where it flowed into the Niger, and from there to the coast of Lagos, where he took a ship to Europe.

The next year found the indefatigable Rohlfs in Egypt. He accompanied the English expedition to Ethiopia and visited the Siwa oasis. And in 1879, he became the first to reveal the secret of another prohibited Saharan city, Cufra, capital of the Senussi religious order.

42 TOP THE GERMAN GUSTAV NACHTIGAL
WAS FASCINATED BY THE LEGENDARY ROCKS
OF THE TIBESTI, THE "ROOF OF THE SAHARA,"
DOTTED WITH PREHISTORIC PAINTINGS. THE
ENGRAVINGS ON THESE TWO PAGES ARE FROM
THE DIARY OF HIS TRAVEL ADVENTURES.

42–43 AFTER CROSSING THE DESERT,
NACHTIGAL WAS CORDIALLY WELCOMED BY
OMAR, THE SULTAN OF BORNU.

43 LEFT During Nachtigal's voyage, the wind whipped up raging sandstorms, often creating dunes as high as hills, at the feet of which the caravan camped.

43 RIGHT Like the explorers who preceded him, Nachtigal also usually dressed in Oriental fashion, passing himself off as a Muslim.

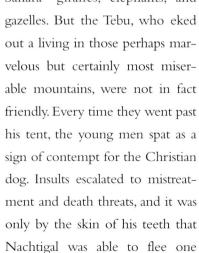

Another German, Gustav Nachtigal, an army doctor who had moved to Tunisia in hopes that the hot African climate would heal his tuberculosis, also crossed still unexplored regions. In 1868 he met Rohlfs in Tunisia. Rohlfs had been appointed by King Wilhelm I of Prussia to bring sultan Omar of the Bornu some gifts and express his gratitude for the help extended to German explorers. Nachtigal, who in the meantime had found his cure, learned Arabic and, becoming increasingly attracted by the perilous lure of the desert, offered to go. He left Tripoli in February 1869, accompanied by Giuseppe Valpreda, an Italian baker, cook, and mechanic who had gone to Africa to seek his fortune. After leaving hospitable Fezzan and reaching Tummo, Nachtigal decided to take advantage of a long forced stay as he waited for a caravan to form in order to cross the most hostile part of the desert, and headed east to explore the Tibesti Mountains, the "Roof of the Sahara," on whose volcanic peaks no European had ever set foot. He found himself in an enchanted world, "an enormous geological whim of titanic architecture with the most incredible formations: cupolas, cathedrals, Byzantine churches, mosques, old castles, mixed with modern constructions in every style. Here the immense back of a camel seems to rise from the earth, there the rocks take on the shape of a gigantic owl; elsewhere, a man's head appears on an isolated column." And in that labyrinth of fairy-tale rocks, ancient paintings of men and animals were scattered here and there, depicting animals now extinct in the Sahara—giraffes, elephants, and gazelles. But the Tebu, who eked out a living in those perhaps marvelous but certainly most miserable mountains, were not in fact friendly. Every time they went past his tent, the young men spat as a sign of contempt for the Christian dog. Insults escalated to mistreatment and death threats, and it was only by the skin of his teeth that Nachtigal was able to flee one

night and return to Murzuch on foot, his food almost gone. He took up his voyage again one year later, in April 1870, and this time went straight across the desert to Kuka, capital of the Bornu, where he was received cordially by sultan Omar, who was surrounded by his armored and helmeted bodyguards.

The German laid at his feet the gifts he had brought from so far away: breech-loading rifles, a reed organ, and a life-size portrait of the king of Prussia. Flattered, the sultan guaranteed hospitality for the travelers. Nachtigal took advantage of it for three years, and Valpreda for the rest of his life, at first voluntarily, then reluctantly, forcefully detained because of his multiple skills. In 1873, after traveling through Bornu, Kanem, and Baghirmi, Nachtigal left for Uadai, the exploration of which, a few years earlier, had cost the life of his compatriot Vogel. Nachtigal had the good fortune to find that its sovereign Alì was brilliant and open-minded, which allowed him to stay for nine months, studying the country and its inhabitants. Finally, having crossed the Darfur, where he stayed another four months—although he found its people "boorish and arrogant"—he reached the Nile at Khartoum. After publishing in Berlin an account of his travels, entitled *Sahara und Sudan,* Nachtigal returned to Africa as the German consul general in Zanzibar, and was subsequently given the task of organizing the territories that would form the German colony of Togo; he died in 1885 on a ship carrying him back home.

Another German, the geologist Oskar Lenz, debunked a fondly held belief of European geographers that the Sahara was the bed of an ancient sea that had dried out millions of years before. Disguised as a Turkish doctor who had joined a caravan, Lenz traveled from Morocco to Timbuktu in 1880. There, he made measurements and observations that led him to conclude that while the desert had once been traversed by numerous rivers, it had never been covered by water. Lenz was the fourth European to set foot in the legendary city. Being a man who loved his comforts, he even brought a mattress with him, along with a profusion of supplies. He was met with an excellent reception, which may have encouraged him to correct the exceptionally negative observations of Caillé and Barth. While it was true that Timbuktu had lost the splendor of its golden years, and its trade now consisted almost solely of ostrich feathers and ivory, thousands of merchants still traveled here during the caravan season. It was governed by a sort of merchant aristocracy that Lenz compared to Venice's, with a doge who here was called a *djema*. The surrounding territory was controlled by the Tuareg to the north and the Fulah to the south, whose rivalry caused a constant state of insecurity and guerrilla warfare. This situation, which greatly harmed business, may have been the reason for a sort of backwards exploration in 1885: the trip to Paris by a so-called envoy of the city. This wiry thirty-year-old, Si El-Hadgi Abd-el Kader, scion of one of the best local families, was self-assured and well educated. He introduced himself to the French authorities of Saint-Louis in Senegal, bearing a message from sheik El-Kraer-Hadgi that the French were welcome to trade with Timbuktu if they so desired. The ambassador was enthusiastically received, introduced to Grévy, president of the

Republic (who was greatly impressed with his long gray beard) and sent back to Senegal with Lieutenant Caron, who was to accompany him to negotiate with the sheik. It was discovered that Kadar did not in fact hold power in the city, and had invented the whole story in order to take power with the help of the French. Caron stayed in Saint-Louis, and the false diplomat, who had had a fine voyage at France's expense, returned home alone, recounting the wonders of what he had seen in Europe.

But the French were nevertheless inexorably encroaching on the edges of the Sahara, and the 1884 Congress of Berlin, convened to divide Africa up among the colonial powers, recognized it as their sphere of influence. To the south, the upper Niger had already been occupied. In 1887, a gunboat under the command of the once disappointed Lieutenant Caron sailed downriver until it came in sight of Cabra, Timbuktu's river port; it did not dock because the area had fallen into anarchy, with continuous battles between the Tuareg and the Fulah. To the north, on the other hand, with Tunisia placed under a protectorate in 1881, France suffered a setback with the massacre of the Flatters mission.

Around 1875, with the Sahara still unconquered and not even fully explored, there was talk of a grandiose project: a trans-Sahara railway that would connect Algeria with Niger and Senegal, absorbing caravan traffic and taming the desert through steam. After all, just a few years earlier, in 1869, the United States connected the Atlantic to the Pacific with iron roads thrusting through the prairies of the Far West, overcoming seemingly insuperable natural obstacles like the Rocky Mountains. Journalists, politicians, dreamers, and engineers published articles, books, and pamphlets until the minister of public works seriously considered

44 LEFT OSKAR LENZ, THE FOURTH EUROPEAN TO VISIT TIMBUKTU, WAS FAVORABLY IMPRESSED BY WHAT HE CONSIDERED A WELCOMING, LIVELY TRADE CITY.

44 CENTER AT THE 1884 CONGRESS OF BERLIN, ORGANIZED BY BISMARCK, COLONIAL POWERS ASSIGNED THE ENTIRE SAHARA TO FRANCE.

44 RIGHT THE MASSACRE OF THE FLATTERS MISSION BY HOGGAR TUAREG IN 1881 PUT A TEMPORARY STOP TO FRENCH EXPANSION IN THE SAHARA.

45 LEFT AND RIGHT FLATTERS WAS ASSIGNED TO STUDY A RAILROAD ROUTE THAT WOULD CONNECT THE MEDITERRANEAN TO THE GULF OF GUINEA.

the matter and appointed a special commission to send the necessary land study missions to the site. One of these was entrusted to Paul Flatters, an Engineers Corps colonel who had already gained some experience in the Sahara by commanding the Laghuat garrison in southern Algeria. In March 1880, Flatters left Biskra, Algeria, with eight other technicians and military personnel and no armed escort for a friendly introduction to the Azger Tuareg, whose leader had been friends with Duveyrier. They surveyed the area up to the northern edge of the Tassili, then returned without completing the work, perhaps because the leader of the Tuareg did not appear at the set time, although they would only have needed to wait a few days. In any event, Flatters departed again at the end of the year, this time following a more western course that was to bring him to the heart of the Hoggar. But the leader of those Tuareg responded with doubt and hostility to his requests for free passage: by now, word that the French wanted to build a railroad had spread throughout the Sahara, and to native peoples this meant subjection and perhaps annihilation. Flatters ignored wise advice and headed out into the desert with eleven technicians and about a hundred Algerian *meharists*—camel "cavalry"—disguised as camel drivers.

His last letter arrived in late January 1881, written from Egéré. Then, for two months there was no news. On March 28, about twenty exhausted men dragged themselves to the gates of Uargla in southern Algeria. They were the expedition's only survivors. Flatters and his men had been attacked in the Sebcha of Amadghor, in the Hoggar, led into an

ambush by about thirty Tuareg who had claimed to be guides sent by their leader. Those not killed immediately met a harsh fate: on foot in the desert, with no food or water, they fell victim to the Tuareg, who had assaulted them near wells and now pretended to be friends, offering them poisoned dates. Some had gone mad, and almost all of them had eaten the bodies of their companions in order to survive.

The tragedy marked the end of the trans-Sahara railroad, and for a good twenty years it put a stop to military expansion as well. But it breathed life into a new myth of the desert: for years there were tales of survivors who had been taken prisoner by the Tuareg. Flatters himself had supposedly been seen in the Hoggar in 1895. According to rumors, he had become one of the veiled men himself, had married and had adopted a daughter.

The massacre indirectly claimed another victim. Those who had dreamed of transforming the Tuareg into linemen for camel railway crossings blamed Duveyrier for their disappointment. His only crime was having described the Tuareg as veiled, turbaned Carolingian paladins; but the explorer was already shaken by the premature death of his fiancée, and embittered by the controversy, he committed suicide in 1892.

A terrible adventure near the Atlantic coast also awaited another desert leader, a young Frenchman who wanted to emulate Caillé's enterprise. Camille Douls was twenty-two years old when he conceived a plan to penetrate one of the still inviolate territories of the Maghreb: Sus in southern Morocco. He chose the most difficult route, landing on the Saharan coast across from the Canary Islands. He spoke Arabic well, had himself circumcised, and masqueraded as an Algerian merchant shipwrecked on that inhospitable shore. When he told this story to the Mauri he met up with, they suspiciously responded that true Muslims came by land; only Christians came by sea. He was overwhelmed, robbed, beaten, and taken to the Mauris' camp, where their leader, Ibrahim, stopped them from slitting his throat, preferring to sell him as a slave. Continuing to claim he was a Muslim, Douls hoped he had gained the friendship of Ibrahim by showing him the place on the coast where he had hidden his goods. He was taken there firmly chained to a camel to avoid any surprises. But as Ibrahim and others abandoned themselves to a dance of predacious joy after opening the boxes, the more ferocious members of the tribe buried Douls up to his neck in the sand and left him there to die,

derisively leaving a jar of water near his lips. Fortunately, Ibrahim found him in time, and Douls had the presence of mind to greet him by reciting the Muslim prayer of the dying, which convinced even the most suspicious that they had been unjustly cruel to one of their own faith. However, to be quite sure, when they returned to camp he was subjected to a close examination of Koranic culture by a holy man, the emir Ma el-Ainin ("Water in the Eyes"). Finally earning the trust of the Mauri, Douls remained with them for five months, joining them in their daily lives, including raids against other tribes that regularly ended in great bloodshed. When Ibrahim made the decision to give him his daughter, the sweet and graceful Eliaziz, as a wife, Douls decided it time to flee. He told Ibrahim that as he had been robbed, he could not pay the traditional dowry, but he had much wealth in Algiers. If someone would guide him to Morocco across the Sus, he could return with gifts worthy of his betrothed. While his beautiful fiancée burst into tears at his departure, Douls secretly exulted as he mounted the camel Ibrahim had given him. After a thousand vicissitudes he reached Marrakech and found a group of English diplomats. He revealed himself to them and was rescued, learning that in France

46 BOTTOM LEFT THE ROCKY DESERT WAS NO LESS IMPERVIOUS THAN THE SANDY ONE, AS WE CAN SEE IN THIS STRETCH OF THE GREAT EASTERN ERG, WHICH THE HORSES AND DROMEDARIES OF FERNAND FOUREAU'S EXPEDITION FACED IN 1897.

46 BOTTOM RIGHT THE EXPLORER FERNAND FOUREAU AND HIS RETINUE HAD TO RELY ON NATIVE COOPERATION AS THEY TRANSFORMED INTO EXPERT CAMEL DRIVERS, COMPETING WITH THE TUAREG IN THEIR ABILITY TO RIDE THE SWIFT MEHARA.

47 LEFT   Timbuktu fell to the French in 1893 and was occupied by a small group of sailors who came down the Niger River on collapsible boats.

47 RIGHT   The bands of Tuareg who controlled the territory around the famous city were attacked and pushed back into the recesses of the desert.

he had been given up for dead.

His terrible experiences did not dim his passion for adventure. Two years later, Douls headed to Timbuktu. Following an extremely unusual itinerary, he left from Suez with a caravan of pilgrims returning from Mecca, but in 1889, after he reached the heart of the Sahara, he was strangled by his Tuareg guides as he was taking a nap. Meanwhile, diplomats were putting the finishing touches on their rough plans to parcel out the African continent. On August 5, 1890, a French-English agreement on setting the boundaries of their respective possessions gave the French a free hand in the west-central Sahara. The British intended it to be a poisoned gift: "So the French cockerel will find something to scratch at," said Lord Salisbury, metaphorically expressing hope that his rivals would become embroiled in long, costly colonial campaigns to bring the immense territory under control. In reality, learning from the hard lesson of the tragic end of Flatters, the French acted with extreme caution. While a detachment of Algerian fusiliers already occupied the El Golea oasis in 1891, before making any further moves, they decided to send out various small scientific expeditions in advance to reconnoiter the land and politically prepare local rulers for annexation. Captain Monteil and his aide Badaire left Saint-Louis in October 1890. With their sixteen Senegalese soldiers (four of whom deserted), they were the first to reach Lake Chad from the west, passing through the Bornu and then crossing the Sahara in the middle of the summer from south to north up to Fezzan and Tripoli, which they reached in December 1892. A follower of Duveyrier's, Fernand Foureau, who had come to the Algerian Sahara as a colonizer, traveled the desert far and wide, pushing in all directions. In fifteen years, he covered about 13,000 miles, a good half of which was in unexplored territory. His numerous contacts with the Tuareg convinced him that these veiled men were not really as terrible as they

seemed, and that a good column of well-armed soldiers could easily subdue them. The first proof that this analysis was correct was the seizure of Timbuktu, which for some time had been controlled by desert horsemen. When Djenné, the great trading city on the Niger, was occupied in 1893, merchants of that city urged the French to push on to Timbuktu. That port of sand, "where pirogue people came face to face with camel people," was the necessary, unavoidable appendage of Djenné, its staple opening to the Sahara. Two columns of French infantry departed, marching along the two banks of the Niger, while a flotilla of steam launches and lighters followed the current, which was especially powerful that year because the rainy season had been especially heavy. Thus, the nineteen sailors arrived at the port of Cabra well ahead of the infantry, and discovered that the unusually high waters had made the ancient channel between Cabra and Timbuktu navigable. They boldly followed it, surprising the city at dawn, entering and fortifying it. They were greeted with joy and hope by merchants weary of the constant bullying of the Tuareg, who had laid siege to the city by setting up ambushes all around its walls. The arrival of French troops on February 12, 1894, freed them from this precarious position. When Colonel Joffre, future marshal during the Great War, took possession of this legendary city in the name of the French Republic, he swept the Tuareg band away from the area with relative ease.

A band of Tuareg took the opportunity to attempt an attack, which was easily repelled. And in late July 1899, Agàdez was occupied and its sultan subdued, with the French flag raised at the palace. Then, during the last stretch of desert, the column risked a mass death when the guides accidentally or intentionally went the wrong way, and they had to return to Agàdez. It was not until November that they arrived in Zinder, where the French learned that their countrymen coming from the Niger had

In 1898, a threefold expedition was organized to connect the still sparse structure of French Africa. Three large columns of soldiers were to converge on Chad to vanquish the reign of the sultan Rabah, a former slave who had taken control of a vast territory in the center of the continent and was desperately opposing European expansion. One column left from the Niger, the second from the Congo, while the third and most important moved out from Uargla in southern Algeria, on October 23, 1898. Their guide was Foureau, who had become a great expert in the Sahara, and Commander Lamy, a war-hardened veteran of various colonial campaigns. There were 306 armed men, Algerian and Saharan and spahi fusiliers, as well as about 80 guides and drivers who were in charge of 1,000 camels loaded with food and munitions. The Tuareg did not dare oppose such an awesome caravan, and allowed it to pass through the gorges of the Hoggar

passed through a few days earlier. On January 21, 1900, they reached the shores of Lake Chad, and in April the three missions finally reunited, a year late. Shortly thereafter they attacked Kusseri, capital of Rabah. Both the sultan and Commander Lamy died during the battle. The French now had a firm hold on the northern and southern zones of the west-central Sahara, but the regions in the middle had barely been touched, and sovereignty over those endless stretches of sand and rock was still only theoretical. Around this time companies of meharists were formed, comprised of expert desert natives commanded by European officials. The troops were perfectly trained to operate in the Sahara, with incursions that led them far from their bases. The principal oases were thus occupied one by one. Having taken the Tademait plateau and Tidikelt, in early 1900 the French installed themselves in In Salah, at the foot of the Hoggar, the mountain massif as large as all of France that was the labyrinthine citadel of

unharmed. Beyond that, near the Inuauen wadi, the French respectfully gathered the remains of the Flatters mission—a few whitened bones. Then, as the camels began to die by the dozens every day, and the men were down to nothing but a handful of dates to eat, they reached Air, where a long stay was necessary in order to find other pack animals and supplies.

the Tuareg. Even though they were feeling increasingly harried, or perhaps because of this, the indomitable veiled warriors did not cease their hostilities and did not change their marauding ways. In 1902, they attacked and raided a large caravan heading to the Tidikelt. The French decided that the time had come to punish them severely. In March 1902, a column of 140 meharists under the

49 Swift and extremely mobile, columns of meharists crossed the Sahara in every direction, traversing the deadliest, most impervious regions and succeeding in subjecting even the last die-hard bands of Tuareg.

command of Lieutenant Cotterest set out from In Salah, on the trail of the raiders.

The French followed them for over a month. Realizing they were being hotly pursued, the Tuareg drew their enemy into more and more desolate areas, hoping they would give up the chase. Finally, the Tuareg tried to set up an ambush. On May 7, near the village of Tit, a few hundred Tuareg attacked the meharists, who barely had time to entrench themselves on a small rise. It was the typical battle of all colonial campaigns: overwhelmingly superior numbers pitted against overwhelmingly superior technology. Modern arms got the better of lances and swords and old shotguns. By the end of the brutal battle, about a hundred Tuareg had fallen, while there were only three dead and ten wounded in the French camp. This disaster marked the end of the military power of the lords of the desert, whose entire forces were no more than three thousand men. Some leaders surrendered immediately, and although most of the tribes still refused to give up, from then on the French were able to travel through the Hoggar with impunity.

As early as October 1902, a column under the command of Lieutenant Gullo-Lohan had penetrated the mountains to cross and map all roads. The next year, the same official was able to begin Saharan mountain climbing by scaling Ilaman, one of its highest peaks, a sheer volcanic cone almost 10,000 feet high. The subjection of one of the most esteemed and courageous leaders, Mussa ag Amastan, appointed *amenokal,* or head of the confeder-

ation of the Hoggar Tuareg, was the final touch to the French push. In 1910, Mussa, accompanied by some of his veiled warriors in their gaudiest costumes, was taken to Paris as a reward for his loyalty. While the Tuareg impressed Parisians with their medieval appearance, they in turn were impressed by France. Upon their return, they described it to their amazed compatriots as "a great garden where peace reigns and not one of the thousands of persons who pass each other on the roads thinks of attacking you or robbing you. You can go about without a saber or dagger." And their fellow countrymen wanted to know whether there were good pastures for camels in Europe. But Mussa and his men could not wait to return to the silence of their desert. While the Hoggar was now completely pacified, many of the most impervious regions still remained independent. To the east, perched on the inaccessible Tassili Mountains with their herds of goats, the Azger Tuareg dared the French by making incursions supported by the Turks, who were still masters of Tripolitania and Cyrenaica and who considered all the central Sahara up to Lake Chad to be their territory. But as one English statesmen cynically remarked, "Colonial expansion cannot be stopped by anything but the presence of a European nation or the sea." Thus, ignoring the protests of the Sublime Gate, in 1905 the French occupied Djanet. They soon had to abandon it, however, pursued as they were by Tuareg guerrilla fighters who could strike and then easily vanish to safety in the Gat oasis in Ottoman territory.

In the far northwest Sahara south of Morocco, the last tongue of desert that still had no white ruler was the stage for two fascinating and little known events that could be considered the swan song of Saharan legend.

On June 12, 1903, in the rectangle of sand and rock overlooking the Atlantic coast between Cape Noun and Cape Bojador, which were described in European chancellery documents as "an uninhabited zone of the Sahara Desert," an expedition appeared that might have changed the course of Saharan history.

The yacht *Frasquita,* with a crew of twenty-six men, dropped anchor near Cape Juby. The owner, Jacques Lebaudy, a French sugar industrialist who a few days earlier had sent a memorandum to his sailors telling them to address him exclusively by the title of Your Majesty, landed with five armed men and took possession of the land for himself and his successors, proclaiming himself Jacques I, Emperor of the Sahara.

Lebaudy traced an outline in the sand that was to delimit the future capital, which he named Troja. He set up two tents, spent his first night in the new empire, and departed the next day, leaving a garrison of five sailors with food for eight days to await the arrival of the prefabricated palace and stables he had ordered from England. The reason for the stables requires a brief explanation: the emperor had rightly noted that horses were not hardy enough for the desert and that camels, a fine example of simplicity, moved too slowly. He thus aimed to create a new animal with the virtues of both, by crossing a fiery purebred with a frugal camel.

Leaving Troja, the *Frasquita* sailed down the coast about fifty miles to a little beach rechristened Polis, where the second city in the empire would be founded. This time, the entire army landed, and they were suddenly confronted by a band of Mauri who had emerged from the dunes. The Mauri unexpectedly decided not to massacre them, but instead trade with them, offering a few slaves to the man who unbeknownst to them was their new "emperor."

Lebaudy refused nobly, but did ask the price of a young Mauri woman, which created something of a stir because the girl was the chief's daughter. Before getting back on the boat, the sovereign had a can of marinated tuna buried on the beach with all due solemnity, as a sign of his perpetual ownership. On June 17, the yacht landed in Las Palmas in the Canary Islands. It hoisted the emperor's white standard with three gold bees, once a Napoleonic symbol of hard work and industriousness, and loaded up foodstuffs to supply Troja. The emperor also took aboard his minister of public works. This man, named Baussy, was to supervise the great works planned: construction of a fort and dock, searching for gold in the sand, and laying a railway from Troja to Timbuktu.

None of it came to pass, because in the meantime the expedition corps had been robbed by the Izerguil tribe, whose *caïd* (who had made a splendid burnoose out of the imperial tent) demanded two thousand francs as a ransom. Offended, Lebaudy turned back to the Canaries, but the other powers had been alarmed by the unexpected appearance of the new "empire," and using sordid legal pretexts, French and Spanish lawyers withdrew permission to sail from the Saharan fleet, which soon thereafter was confiscated and sold at auction.

Lebaudy then left for Holland, with the goal of presenting his case to the International Court at The Hague. He later settled in London, appointed other ministers, enlisted volunteers, published the *Journal Officiel de l'Empire du Sahara,* spent hundreds of thousand of francs, began negotiations with the English, Turks, and

51 LEFT In 1903, the yacht *Frasquita* disgorged the strangest expedition that had ever touched African soil: the French sugar industrialist Jacques Lebaudy and his followers.

51 RIGHT Landing on the only area of the continent that was not yet under European domination, Lebaudy proclaimed himself emperor of the Sahara.

Moroccans, entered into a rather undiplomatic correspondence with his royal "cousins," and finally decided to check himself into a New York mental hospital. He escaped a few years later and decided to emulate a practice of ancient Peruvian and Egyptian dynasties by marrying his fourteen-year-old daughter. His wife shot him dead with a revolver.

After Lebaudy's ephemeral and rather frivolous dream faded, a new mirage arose within his former empire that attracted, disquieted, and excited the restless Europeans. In 1899, near the Sahara wadi (a dry streambed) known as Seguiet el-Hamra, an invisible holy city was founded. In just a few years it stirred up the improbable, miraculous legend of Smara the inaccessible, the Gorgon of the desert. It was the brainchild of the emir Ma el-Ainin, whom we encountered earlier as he was interrogating poor Douls on the Koran. His intent was to found a cultural and religious center for Mauri nomads. His prestige, fame, and devotion made it easy for him to obtain all the necessary construction material from the sultan of Morocco, except for sand and rocks, which were available on site. For months, dozens of xebecs unloaded wood and plaster, masons and decorators, foodstuffs and seeds, at the mouth of Seguiet el-Hamra. The famous mosaics of Mogador arrived on muleback. The most celebrated architect in Morocco came to direct the work. Wells were dug and a date grove was planted. The casbah was comprised of eighteen edifices that surrounded the emir's residence. High gates opened within the walls so that the camels that carried the women of Ma el-Ainin and his followers could enter with the immense canopy, or baldachin. All around, houses and warehouses sprang up to accommodate the nomads who gathered in Smara to hear the world of God and sell captured slaves or stolen goods. Disciples came from all over the Sahara. Mauri raiders came to exchange the fruits of their assaults on caravans and plot new raids. The newly founded city rapidly became both a fable and a nightmare. To the Europeans who barely controlled the country, it was, for over a decade, a symbol of the elu-sive, ubiquitous ghosts of the desert. To natives, it was a citadel of faith and an oasis of delights: its waters, gardens, mosques, mosaics, women, wares, ascetics, and veiled and unveiled warriors created an oral tradition with countless legends that spread throughout the entire Sahara: that it had been built in a single night by the *djinn,* evil spirits that had been imprisoned and forced to complete that holy task by the power of Ma el-Ainin; behind its walls, beautiful maidens awaited the boldest and luckiest raiders; if the infidels neared it, the *simùn,* the harsh desert wind, would rise, burying them under waves of sand.

Lieutenant Mouret, a young French official who at that time was the commissioner of Mauritania, was the one who in part destroyed that vast edifice of the imagination. In 1913, the massacre of one of his detachments by the Mauri exasperated him enough to commit a folly: he crossed more than six hundred miles of total desert with four hundred men and nine officials. After a terrible three-week march, the expedition reached Smara. The nomads, perhaps trusting in the simùn, had abandoned the city to vanish among the dunes and rocks. To avoid any possible trap, Mouret did not even enter his coveted and hated destination. He pointed his cannons and ordered it to be razed to the ground. The Mauri still recount that great Smara burned for days and days. As its infinite treasures burned, the smoke from the fire rose in a column that covered the sky and was seen by all the dismayed tribes.

THE LAST ADVENTURERS

Still, the legend of the desert capital survived. By 1930, no European had yet managed to set foot there. That year, twenty-five-year-old Michel Vieuchange, dressed as an Arab woman, left from French Morocco to conquer that little white spot that still remained on the map of the world. But an encounter with a band of marauders forced him to turn back. Vieuchange did not give up. He set off again a few weeks later and, hidden in a bag hanging off the side of a camel, crossed a field of three thousand tents of fanatical nomad rebels. Still in that uncomfortable position, he finally entered the forbidden city, or at least its ruins. He walked along a few streets, took a hundred and fifty photos (all out of

focus), and came to safety after a harsh march through the desert, only to die a few days later, struck down by a violent attack of dysentery. Only in 1936 did that white spot finally get its flag: the Spanish officially occupied what until then had been only a nominal possession. Its name taken from old Portuguese nautical maps, the colony was called Rio de Oro, although there were scarce traces of any river and none of gold. A few years earlier, in 1931, another holy city of the Sahara had fallen. White Cufra in the Libyan desert, the home of the Islamic religious brotherhood of the Senussi, was seized by the Italians. Although they had taken

Tripolitania and Cyrenaica from the Turks in 1911, the Arab revolt had forced them to limit their occupation to the coastal area. Only after the Great War were they able to slowly resume their advance toward the inland oases, getting as far as Gadàmes in 1924, Giarabùb in 1926, Fezzan in 1929, and Gat in 1930. After taking Cufra as well, a vast exploratory campaign began. Over the course of a decade, numerous missions crossed every part of the Libyan Sahara to Tibesti, studying every aspect of the country. The numerous prehistoric rock paintings that were discovered provided a quite unexpected and fascinating account of the Sahara's distant past. In the 1920s and 1930s, the unknown region from the Nile to the Tibesti and Ennedi mountains was also explored. A young Egyptian diplomat, Ahmed Mohamed bey Hassanein, who had already accompanied the adventurous English traveler Rosita Forbes to the still inviolate Cufra in the winter of 1920–1921, departed in January 1923 from the little port of Sollùm, on the Libyan-Egyptian border, to push farther and farther south to the unknown mountains of Archenu and Auenàt, which had only been visited from time to time by Tebu shepherds of distant Tibesti in search of pastures. Hassanein hoped to discover the lost oases of Zarzura, of which the nomads of Egypt and Libya told tales. He thought he had found them among those peaks: "One morning, a few minutes before dawn, after crossing a number of steep dunes, we suddenly saw, from the summit of the last dune, a distant mountain range hidden in the fog, with the profile of an ancient feudal castle. A few moments later, the sun suddenly rose on the horizon, flooding those gray mountains with pink light. And letting the caravan go ahead of me, I sat on the dune contemplating those mountains that until

then I had thought were non-existent legends, the barrier that rose before the valleys of the first of the lost oases." Another Egyptian, prince Husein Kemal-el-Din, set out to fill the remaining gaps in the map of those regions, which he accurately completed in repeated expeditions from 1923 to 1929. The Hungarian count Ladislao Almasy tenaciously pursued the phantom oasis of Zarzura. In 1933, he was sure he had found it in the verdant wadis of Abd el Melik, among the mountains of Gilf Kebir north of the Auenàt not far from Cufra. But the elusive Zarzura with its gardens remained in the geography of dreams and Saharan mirages.

To the west, after having abandoned some positions during the Great War due to the rebellion of various nomadic tribes that had been incited to holy war by the Senussi and Turkey, which was an ally of Germany, the French had completed their exploration of the immense slice of the Sahara they had received when the colonial pie was divided. In 1913, just prior to the conflict, Captain Cortier had crossed the most terrible part, the Tanezruft, "the land of fear." It was about sixty square miles of pebbles, with no wells or vegetation. The 1920s brought the expeditions of Captain Augiéras and the naturalist Théodore Monod to the Mauri Sahara. In 1936, Monod would be the first to cross the Tanezruft at its widest point. In addition to numerous scientific volumes, he would write the most poetic book on the allure of the Sahara: *Meharée,* published in 1937 and dedicated "to the camel and the water-bag, the vehicle and the container, the only winners in the desert." In reality, when Monod wrote this, another winner of the Sahara could have been a mechanical mode of transport. While steam had not been able to conquer the desert solitudes, and the trans-Sahara railway had been relegated to the illusions of nineteenth-century scientific vainglory, the internal combustion engine had become the camel's most formidable enemy. The first attempts to use the automobile to cross the Sahara, by Colonel Joseph Laperrine d'Hautpoul, another great figure in turn-of-the-century explorations, occurred between 1917 and 1919. Laperrine, who had crossed the entire stretch from Uargla to the Hoggar and back by car, wanted to accomplish the same feat by airplane, and in 1920 made the first attempt to cross the

Sahara by air. It ended tragically. A squadron of five airplanes at his command left from Biskra on February 7, with the goal of reaching Timbuktu and then Dakar. The flight took place in stages, given the very limited autonomy of aircraft of the time, and followed caravan routes. By the time they reached Tamanrasset only two of the five aircraft were able to continue. They took off together on February 20, but Laperrine's airplane was sucked into a sandstorm, lost its bearings, and was forced to land in the middle of the desert, where it overturned. Although he was seriously injured, the commander and the two mechanics who accompanied him attempted to reach the oasis of Tin Zuaten, which he thought was quite near. It was actually more than a hundred miles away, and after walking about twenty miles, the exhausted men decided to return to the wreckage of the airplane and wait for help. They had the water from the radiator and a small amount of food supplies, but the days passed and their hopes grew ever dimmer. On March 5, Laperrine died. Another nine days passed before a column of meharists finally found the two survivors, now near death. The commander's body was brought to Tamanrasset, in the Hoggar he had loved so much, to be buried next to the heart of another extraordinary figure who had loved the Sahara: his friend Charles de Foucault. Foucault, a scion of a great aristocratic French family and a cavalry officer, had in 1883–1884 traversed the unknown routes of the Moroccan Sahara disguised as a Jewish merchant. When he discovered his religious vocation, he abandoned his wealth and honors to become a missionary. In 1905, after wandering through various monasteries in the Near East, he settled in Tamanrasset, "in the most beautiful hermitage in the world, on the summit of a mountain in the middle of the Hoggar, surrounded by a fabulous scene of peaks and rocky spires." His intention was not so much to convert the Tuareg, whose customs and language he was studying, as to live in mystic solitude closer to God in that desert that the Arabs rightly called "the Garden of Allah." After he was killed in 1916 by a group of rebels who believed he was hiding arms in his tiny dry-stone monastery, his body was removed to France, except for his heart, which was placed in a small urn in the little chapel he had built with his own hands.

The incursions of Laperrine and other French officials had shown that while the automobile might be a good substitute for the camel ("with the combined aid of boards, shovels, draught animals and elbow grease," wrote an exhausted driver), it had an enormous weak spot: tires.

The problem was resolved through the use of caterpillar treads, thanks to which five half-track Citroën automobiles were able to complete the first automobile crossing of the Sahara, led by Georges-Marie Haardt, general manager of Usines Citroën, and his second in command Louis Audouin-Dubreuil. They left from Tuggurt on December 17, 1922, and reached Timbuktu on January 10, 1923. They celebrated Christmas in the Hoggar. The Hoggar Tuareg they met were not at all impressed by the vehicles, in which they solemnly took a seat for a short ride "as if they had been doing this all their lives." They were, however, quite impressed by the expedition's mascot, a furry little dog that they mistook for a "dwarf ram." The enterprise, followed in 1924–1925 by another journey, when the same men crossed Africa from Algeria to Cape Town, marked the beginning of a new era. A few years later, in 1938, the *Shell Guide* could already claim: "In this region the Sahara has now become a popular place for automobile and airplane tourism."

With geographic reconnaissance complete, prospecting came next. The Sahara proved to have a wealth of minerals: iron, coal, manganese, copper, tin, uranium, and above all oil, whose discovery in the 1950s changed the face of many areas of the desert and radically transformed the economic situation of a number of countries. Unfortunately, during this period the "Garden of Allah" became a gigantic firing range for France's

54 A COLUMN OF HALF-TRACKS DOES RECONNAISSANCE ALONG A ROAD IN SOUTHERN ALGERIA IN 1930. CATERPILLAR TREADS WERE WHAT ALLOWED VEHICLES TO CROSS THE SAHARA FOR THE FIRST TIME.

54–55 THE MISSION CITROËN, LED BY GEORGES-MARIE HAARDT AND LOUIS AUDOUIN-DUBREUIL, LEFT TUGGURT AND REACHED TIMBUKTU IN TWENTY-FOUR DAYS, CROSSING 2,175 MILES OF DESERT AT AN AVERAGE SPEED OF THIRTY MILES AN HOUR: IT WAS A FIRST FOR THIS INCREDIBLY RUGGED TERRAIN.

56 RIGHT The Mission Citroën had an enormous impact and was used by the automobile company to advertise its vehicles. The playbill shown here publicized the documentary made of the expedition.

56–57 One of the Citroën weasels used on the memorable Black Crossing, which traversed the entire African continent, is ferried across a river in Oubanghi-Chari.

56 LEFT With the proud, stiff pose of true Sahara conquerors, Haardt and Audouin-Dubreuil, binoculars and maps on hand, gaze out at their distant destination.

missiles and nuclear experiments, which finally ended with Algerian independence. Despite the development of several regions during the second half of the twentieth century, the fate of the Sahara has not been happy. After decolonization, the desert was parceled out to various nations that were the heirs of European powers, and carved into countries whose borders made no sense and showed no regard for the economic situation and interests of the people, especially the nomads. As a result, the desert has seen the rise of new conflicts, like that between Libya and Chad for possession of the Tibesti, and the Mauri war of independence in the former Spanish colony of Rio de Oro, which was coveted by Morocco. But the real tragedy seems to be the accelerating process of desertification caused by climate changes underway across the planet, which has helped dry up some oases and expand the desert sand to the Sahel region.

HORIZONS OF SAND

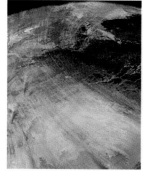
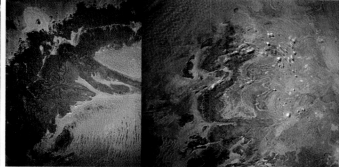

58 LEFT TO RIGHT AND 59 Mineral striation in a rock in the Acacus Mountains of Libya; the rocky labyrinth of Tadrart Acacus; oasis in Chad; Gebel Indinen in the Acacus; dunes in the Libyan desert.

60 The remote plateau of Gilf Kebir in the western Egyptian desert on the border of Libya and Sudan can be seen in the foreground in this satellite view. In the background we can see the Nile and the Sinai Peninsula.

61 TOP LEFT The volcanic buttresses of the Tibesti emerge like an island in a sea of sand. We can see the lines of dry riverbeds, or *ENNERI*, merging with the desert and finally vanishing (LEFT).

61 TOP CENTER The cloudless sky clearly sets off one of the features of the Algerian Sahara—the fossil beds of the wadi.

61 TOP RIGHT The remains of vast, tabular plateaus with eroded, crumbling edges emerge in a flat expanse of sand partially covered by dunes.

61 BOTTOM Photographed from an altitude of 250 miles, Lake Chad reveals its jagged, vague outlines, partially invaded by the sand.

ANATOMY OF A DESERT

An immense expanse of sand, stones, and desolate plains where there is nothing as far as the eye can see. Merciless temperatures that fluctuate from 120°F in summer to −10°F in winter. A tormented land, swept by implacable winds and dust storms that can swallow up entire armies. Mysterious, bare mountains and vestiges of prehistoric geological catastrophes. A desert—the king of all deserts—that until a few thousand years ago was a prairie, irrigated by mighty rivers and lakes as large as the Caspian Sea. The Sahara, the antithesis of life, where the rain never falls and water is a mirage reflected from the sky. A place of paradoxes and miracles, of animals who have learned not to drink, plants that sprout and die in one day, underground fish, and lizards that swim in the sand. A paradise lost, where survival is an art, a tiptoe dance.

The Sahara is the largest desert on Earth. It extends from the Atlantic coast to the Red Sea and from the Mediterranean to black Africa, 3,000 miles long and almost 1,300 miles wide. It covers over a quarter of the African continent. The immense land is absolutely arid. The Sahara is a realm of rock and inorganic matter, an enormous battlefield in which all life has been destroyed. For hundreds and hundreds of miles, there is not a blade of grass, a bush, or a tree worthy of the

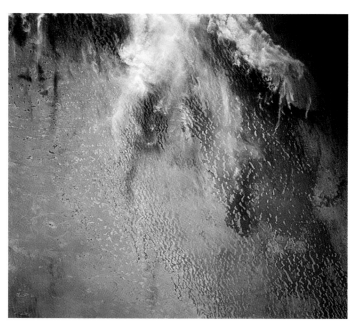

name. It is a cosmic void that gives a traveler the uneasy sensation of being on another planet.

Yet this enormous expanse of barren earth that makes up the Sahara is anything but uniform and monotonous. The Sahara system is like a petrified organism, comprised of totally different macroenvironments. Yet rather than being mutually exclusive, these environments permeate and balance one another. Depressions that sink to below sea level are succeeded by great massifs that may be as much as 10,000 feet high. Enormous mounds of sand alternate with *hammadas*, flat, rocky expanses covered with stones and broken slabs of rock. The integrating element that unites and connects the desert's different manifestations is the fossil hydrographic network: a colossal web of dried rivers, lost forever to the sea, dried lakes full of sediments whose dry surfaces hide water, a tangle of water tables and tiny underground streams. Its presence or absence has drastically influenced economic subsistence models, has guided migrations and commercial routes, and has established the form and quality of human settlements. In the Sahara, we can rightfully speak of a geography of thirst. Just take a look at a map, and you will see how extensive and yet completely disorganized the river system is. The basin of Lake Chad covers about 880,000 square miles, extending from the Hoggar and Air Mountains to the slopes of the Tibesti. But of this immense web, only a portion is active, just 40 percent of its potential; today, Lake Chad is no more than twenty-three feet deep and is fed exclusively by the Logoné River, which draws its sustenance from the rainy regions of central Africa. Its other tributaries and distributaries are practically inactive. The ancient valley trough across the Teneré is completely unrecognizable, submerged and obstructed by enormous masses of sand. To the west of the Air Mountains, the effect of aridity on the hydrographic system is even more sensational: the Azaouak valley, many miles wide and almost 1,000 miles long, reveals the past existence of a mighty river that joined the Niger near present-day Niamey. Today, at least in its northern course, the Azaouak is completely covered by sand, and only satellite images reveal its traces.

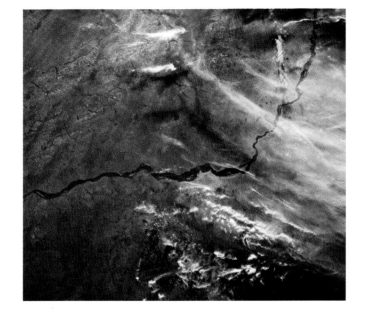

With some simplification, we can distinguish three primary zones in the Sahara, each one with its own characteristics: the western, central, and eastern Sahara. The first is delimited to the north by the Atlas Mountains and to the south by the Hoggar Mountains, extending from the Atlantic coast to the border of Libya. This is the Sahara of the great oases, which line the courses of dried rivers or rest on the slopes of enormous dune systems. But the western Sahara is also a place where the desert shows its most hostile face, with endless stretches of completely barren land and oceans of tangled, practically impassable dunes that cover an area as large as northern Italy, making up the Great Western Erg, the Great Eastern Erg, and the Chech Erg. The central portion of the Sahara has imposing mountain massifs that are the remains of ancient volcanoes. These mountains—the Hoggar, the Tassili n'Ajjer, the Tibesti, and the Ennedi—and their offshoots cover an immense square area between the Algerian *reg* and the Libyan desert. In the Hoggar and the Tibesti,

the desert expresses itself in altitude: the peak of Assekrem in Atakor is 9,500 feet high, and the peaks of Emi Koussi, the highest point of the Tibesti and the entire Sahara, are more than 11,000 feet above sea level. East of the Tibesti is the so-called Libyan desert, which in reality includes vast portions of Sudan, Chad, and Egypt. The eastern Sahara has no mountains worthy of note, but rather a shield of small tables gently sloping down to the Mediterranean. The geomorphology of the Libyan desert, practically void of river valleys, is characterized by vast, deep depressions with steep walls. The one at Qattara, west of Cairo, is known as the Devil's Lair and drops 430 feet below sea level. The oases in the Libyan desert are sparse and isolated, distant from each other and connected by faint caravan tracks that are difficult to travel. The Libyan desert is the least populated zone of the Sahara. Here, the Latin term *desertus* ("abandoned place") expresses itself most clearly. The Nile is the great exception in the eastern Sahara. As we survey the region, it is impossible not to marvel at the contrast between the Nile and the Sahara, the metaphysical, extreme union of opposites. The Nile originates in the heart of the great lakes in equatorial Africa, where the rain is abundant and generally falls all year round. The river thus departs well equipped for its long voyage to the Mediterranean. And yet, even with the contribution of the Blue Nile, even this enormous quantity of water from the equatorial mountains would not be sufficient to cross the desert. Like the Niger, when the Nile has traveled about a third of its course, it comes to an inland delta, the Sudd: for some time the river loses itself in this basin, 31,000 square miles in size, and is invaded by marsh grasses as it wanders through thousands of channels and blind offshoots. When it flows out of the Sudd, the Nile has lost half its capacity. The river survives its crossing of the Sahara only due to the conformation of its valley,

64 A TINY SOLITARY CLOUD CASTS A SHADOW ON THE IMMENSE EXPANSE OF DUNES THAT EXTENDS ACROSS A VAST BASIN IN THE LIBYAN DESERT IN EGYPT.
THE AREA ENDS IN A BROAD AMPHITHEATER OF GREATLY ERODED TABLES, NEAR THE CENTER, WHICH ARE IN TURN DELIMITED BY AN AREA OF MORE JAGGED RISES.
COUNTLESS DRIED-UP RIVERBEDS DEEPLY FURROW THE HILLS.

65 THE LIBYAN DESERT, HERE PHOTOGRAPHED IN EGYPT, IS GENERALLY FLAT; THE BEDS OF FOSSIL WATERWAYS ARE EXTREMELY SHORT (LEFT)
AND THE HILLS ARE MOSTLY TABLES THAT ARE RATHER MODEST IN SIZE AND ELEVATION (RIGHT).

perhaps the most ancient river valley on Earth. The entire course of the Sahara Nile is in fact enclosed within a sort of deep natural channel bounded by walls of solid rock, which prevents the dispersion of water. The fate of its tributaries, north of the 16th parallel, is quite different: all traces of the hydric network have completely vanished, erased under faceless plains smoothed by the wind.

To the south, the Sahara dissolves into the Sahel, which in Arabic means "shore," a transition area between the savanna and the bare lands of the north. The Sahel extends across a broad swath of territory, cutting across the African continent from the Atlantic to the Red Sea. A rain gauge shows the Sahel receives between 10 and 24 inches of rainfall, but in reality the break with the desert is not so clear. Two large rivers, the Senegal and the Niger, flow through long tracts of the western section of this area, changing its features. It is a vague, fluctuating border that straddles two different worlds.

The astounding variety of Sahara landscapes is accompanied by a uniform geological structure. The Sahara in fact consists entirely of a very ancient rocky shelf, a platform of crystalline schist, granite, and ancient volcanic rock. Over time, this base has undergone endless processes of flattening and erosion, and was almost totally covered with sediments. It emerges significantly only in the Hoggar and Tibesti Mountains. The accumulation of sedimentary surfaces, which makes the Sahara essentially flat, also created the table-shaped plateaus that in another form are one of the most significant features of the Sahara landscape: Tassili n'Ajjer in Algeria is one of the most spectacular examples of these formations. Finally, the drastic reduction of precipitation, the reason for the more recent process of desertification, allowed the wind to act with all its force. The wind is the primary cause of the Sahara's present-day appearance: not only the bizarre form of the rocks, but also the accumulations of sand, great ergs and barchans, or shifting, crescent-shaped dunes. The grains of sand move according to a process called "saltation": lifted by the wind, they fol-

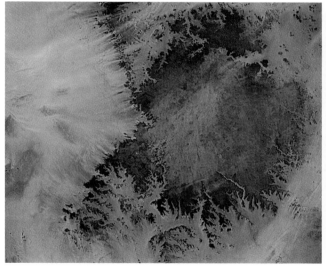
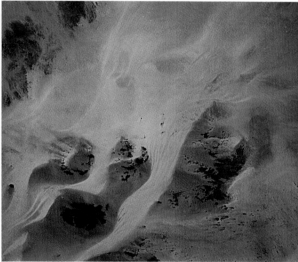

low a short parabolic trajectory, then bounce onto the ground, where they move other grains. This mechanism of action-reaction can lead to the formation either of the typical wrinkles that furrow the Sahara plains, causing them to resemble the ocean floor, or of dunes of varying sizes. All it takes is a significant obstacle, a change in the wind or temperature, and the process can expand in unpredictable directions and measures. Sahara terminology to distinguish the various dune forms is extremely vast: in addition to barchans, there are saber-shaped *sifs, draas* (sand ridges that may be as high as 1,000 feet), and *rhourds,* or star-shaped dunes. For a Sahara traveler, either on camelback or in a motor vehicle, the dunes are a nightmare: in the hypnotizing chaos of an *aklé,* a barchan arranged in parallel ridges with various intersections, it is easy to become disoriented, often with tragic results. One moves through the dunes by seeking sand-free corridors, where they exist: some of these passages were used for centuries by the caravans, and served as entryways for explorers, pioneers, and invading armies. Many of the paved roads that now cross the Sahara follow the traces of these providential gaps. Although dear to the collective imagination of civilized humankind, the image of a Sahara covered with dunes is inaccurate: sandy areas in fact account for only 20 percent of the desert's surface. Romantic spirits must resign themselves to the harsh reality: most of the Sahara is occupied by dismal plains, mountains calcified by the sun, and horrible stone fields.

Atlantic Ocean

MAGHREB

MOROCCO

SAHARA ATLAS

Tahert (Tiaret)

Sedrata

T

Touggourt

GREAT WESTERN ERG

Rissani (Sijilmassa)

Ouargla

MZAB

TUAT

TADEMAIT PLATEAU

GREAT EASTERN ERG

Timimoun

Adrar

In Salah

Aoulef

Reggane

TIDIKELT

Arak

AMADROR

TA

N'A

ERG CHECK

ALGERIA

WESTERN SAHARA

Idjil

TANEZROUFT

Mt. Assekrem

HOGGAR

Tamanrasset

Ouadane

Taoudeni

Atar

Mt. Greboun

Wadi Tafassasset

MAURITANIA

Araouane

AïR

MALI

Arlit

Teguiddam Tessoun

Bagza Mounte

Tichitt

Aoudaghost

In Gall

Agadez

HODH

Oualata

Ménaka

SAHEL

Timbuktu

Gao

TAHOUA

NIGER

Mopti

Niger River

Niamey

Djenné

San

SENEGAL

M e d i t e r r a n e a n S e a

NISIA

○ Tripoli

○ Ghadames

L I B Y A

Qattara
Depression

Cairo ○

○ Siwa
oasis

El-Faiyum
oasis

L I B Y A N   D E S E R T

ILI
ER

FEZZAN

Murzuq

E G Y P T

Ghat

Jabal Bin
Ghanimah

El-Kharga
oasis

Nile

ACACUS

janet

Cufra
oasis

EASTERN DESERT

Djado

TIBESTI

TENERE

Séguédine

ERDI

lakes of
Ounianga

Emi Koussi

Mourdi
Depression

S U D A N

ree of
énéré

Bilma

Faya ○

ENNEDI

Fachi

Fada ○

C H A D

Khartoum ○

Bahr el-Ghazal

KORDOFAN

DARFUR

Lake Chad

Yo ○

○ Logoné

SUDD

68 THE HARSH CLIMATE OF TADRART ACACUS IN THE WESTERNMOST PART OF LIBYA IS A RELATIVELY RECENT CONDITION; IN THE 4TH MILLENNIUM B.C. THE REGION WAS EXTREMELY FERTILE AND INHABITED BY ADVANCED PEOPLES.

69 LEFT THE SAHARA'S ARIDITY WAS AGGRAVATED BY DROUGHT IN THE 1970s: BOTH WILD AND DOMESTICATED FLORA AND FAUNA, WHICH WERE ALREADY RARE, DECREASED SO MUCH THAT VARIOUS SPECIES WERE BROUGHT TO THE VERGE OF EXTINCTION.

69 RIGHT AS IF IN MEDITATION, A SAHARA NOMAD CONTEMPLATES ONE OF THE FEW PERMANENT WATER HOLES IN THE WESTERN SAHARA. WATER IS BEYOND A DOUBT THE MOST PRECIOUS COMMODITY IN THE DESERT, WHERE RAIN IS INCREDIBLY RARE AND DROUGHTS CAN GO ON FOR YEARS, PUTTING BOTH HUMAN AND ANIMAL LIFE AT RISK.

AN ARID HEART

Over various geological eras, the Sahara experienced continuously alternating moist and arid periods, with drastic climate changes due to various factors: continental drift, advancing and retreating glaciers, marine transgression, and changes in atmospheric circulation. The so-called dinosaur cemetery in Gadafoua, one of the most desolate regions of Niger, shows how broad the fluctuations of this pendulum can be (even over much shorter periods): where the Teneré now stretches, 200 million years ago rain forests flourished, a luxuriant world traversed by broad rivers and dotted with water holes. As we gradually reach present times, and we gain more information on the Sahara's past, the pattern becomes clearer, enough to allow us to attempt a reliable reconstruction of events. Climate changes are not clear and constant, but fluctuate until they cross a threshold. Something similar must have happened in the Sahara, where the collapse of ecosystems was probably preceded by significant fluctuations in climate. The most likely hypothesis is that in different regions of the Sahara there were different climate conditions that followed the glacial periods, with perhaps significant variations from one area to another. During the Pleistocene, the Sahara was certainly scattered with large bodies of fresh water, whose expansion and contraction followed surprisingly rapid rhythms, with a dizzying finale. The fluctuations of Lake Chad provide a more than exhaustive example of the evolution of the Sahara over the past 20,000 years. At that time the Sahara climate began to deteriorate rapidly and inexorably, and the desert expanded well beyond its present-day boundaries, advancing to almost the 10th parallel. Dunes formed 300 miles south of their present-day limit,

all the way to the rain forest. Lake Chad, which during the previous wet period had been about 135,000 square miles in size, gradually shrank to somewhere around its present dimensions. Then, a new influx of moisture moved in, followed by an interval of drought. Finally, around 12,000 years ago, the desert's offensive seemed to fade, the sands retreated, and the rain once again fell abundantly. Lake Chad expanded again, transforming into a true inland sea as large as the Caspian. The decline began about 4,000 years ago, when the desert finally triumphed for good. Of course, this scheme is not accurate for every region of the Sahara: the regions east of the Tibesti were experiencing persistent drought, with weak, irregular precipitation reckoned to be on average barely four inches a year. What is certain is that the process of desertification occurred over an extremely short period, just a few thousand years. Paleoclimatologists believe that the cause of this swift catastrophe was the change in sunlight due to the shifting rotation of the Earth's axis. Indeed, the monsoon front, the only real hope of rain, has now retreated well to the south, too far to influence the dominant aridity. An extremely efficient atmospheric system has settled over the Sahara and gathered strength, based on a permanent high pressure area that occupies the center. This functions like an enormous fan that takes the moist air from the Atlantic and Mediterranean and blows it out toward the edge of the desert.

The winds that sweep the Sahara, like the scirocco, the khamsin, and the harmattan, are dusty, hot, and implacable and blow from the center of the desert out. Like the djinn, demons that nomads believe inhabit the empty space, they seem pervaded by a hellish fury: their task is to defend the edges of the Sahara, push back the clouds that could bring rain, and maintain the climate's status quo. The absence of vegetation and the leveling of the landscape interact with powerful, ceaseless winds in a vicious cycle that perpetuates impossible living conditions. The harmattan can blow constantly for two months straight, pervading the landscape with a sort of dense, heavy mineral fog. These clouds of dust particles (lithometeors) can be gigantic, covering hundreds of square miles. Sometimes, especially in the late spring, the Sahara is whipped by true sandstorms, which can reach an incredible power. The sun vanishes, hidden behind a reddish curtain, and visibility is reduced to just a few yards. Life stops, as if in the clutches of a supernatural paralysis. Those who live in the desert fear these storms, and stories told around their campfires contain a litany of terrifying episodes: caravans lost, animals killed, tents swept away and buried under the sand with all their occupants. Sometimes dust clouds from the Libyan and Algerian deserts can reach southern Europe and beyond, sprinkling the glaciers of the Italian and Swiss Alps with a fine dusting of sand.

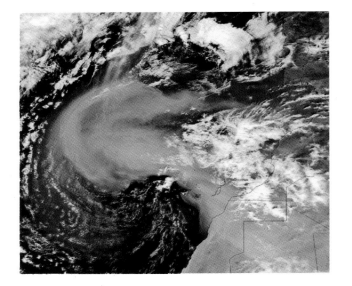

Real rain in the Sahara is an extremely rare and fortuitous event. Rain only comes by accident, when the monsoon front manages to break past the compact shield of Sahara high pressure areas. In addition, the almost total lack of clouds and mist results in strong sunlight, which aggravates dry conditions. In Tamanrasset, at the foot of the Hoggar, there are at least 310 days of sun every year; and in Adrar, in the Algerian Tuat, the sun blazes down 340 days a year; in Gao, in the Mali Sahel, it drops to 275 days a year, which is little consolation (Paris and Milan have 140 days of sun a year). Moreover, in the Sahara the sunlight is much stronger than in temperate regions. Not even elevation, which usually influences the quantity and quality of pre-

cipitation, has any significant effect. In the Tibesti, 10,000 feet high, it rains only about four inches, or 100 millimeters, a year. Consulting the Sahara rain gauge is an exercise in statistical horror. Here are the average values in millimeters for some localities: Cufra (southeastern Libya) 1.9; Reggane (Erg Chech, Algeria) 5.8; Bilma (Teneré, Niger) 22; Faya (Tibesti, Chad) 5. Even more than scarcity, irregularity is what distinguishes the Sahara climate system: some areas of the Libyan desert have not seen a drop of rain for twelve consecutive years (Kharga, Egypt, was dry for seventeen years!). Excesses apart, "normal" intervals between one rainfall and another are still depressing: between seven and fourteen months in the central Sahara and between six and nine months in southern regions. Sometimes the air is so hot and dry that raindrops do not even manage to complete their fall, evaporating a few yards from the ground. All Sahara travelers are quite familiar with this frustrating phenomenon: looking up, they can see the rain, smell it, and almost touch it with their hands, but cannot benefit from it. To be useful, precipitation must be over 5 millimeters (about a quarter of an inch) and fall within a twenty-four-hour period; this is the only way the soil can retain enough moisture to permit the growth of vegetation. But it does not always happen. The nomads of the Sahara are well aware of this, and insufficient rainfall is not even recorded in the calendar of oral tradition, repeated like a propitiatory liturgy during dry periods. It is thus no surprise that in all Sahara languages, rain (and water in general) is related to the divine and spiritual: for the nomads of Mauritania it is *rahma*, the Mercy of Allah, a rare and precious gift. Yet when the drought is over and it finally rains, disaster may result. In 1922, Tamanrasset was almost completely destroyed by a cloudburst that caused dozens of deaths; the same thing happened in Murzuch,

72–73 GREAT BARCHANS RISE IN THE AREA BETWEEN THE TADRART ACACUS ESCARPMENT, STANDING OUT IN THE BACKGROUND, AND WADI MATANDUS. GIVEN THE EXTREME CONDITIONS, THE REGION IS PRACTICALLY UNINHABITED: ONLY A FEW FAMILIES OF AZGHER TUAREG MANAGE TO LIVE IN THIS DESOLATION, ALTHOUGH IT IS FILLED WITH A MAGNIFICENT, NAMELESS BEAUTY.

73 LEFT   THE MYSTERIOUS METEORITE THAT ACCORDING TO TRADITION IS STILL AWAITING ITS DISCOVERER IN THE DESERTS OF MAURITANIA MAY RESEMBLE THIS ROCKY FORMATION, A SIMPLE CALCAREOUS OUTCROPPING ERODED BY THE WIND.

73 RIGHT   THE FORCE OF THE WIND, ALONG WITH THE INFILTRATION OF NIGHTTIME HUMIDITY AND THE BRUTAL ALTERNATION OF COLD AND HEAT, CONSTANTLY AND METICULOUSLY CRUMBLE THE SANDSTONE OF TADRART ACACUS, SHAPING IT INTO AN INFINITE ARRAY OF FORMS AND CREATING HONEYCOMB PATTERNS, SPIRES, GROTTOS, AND NATURAL SHELTERS.

74–75   IN THE IMMENSE PLAIN, A MAN FACES A CLOUD OF DUST ABOUT TO SWALLOW HIM UP. SAND- AND DUST STORMS ARE FREQUENT IN THE SAHEL, ESPECIALLY IN THE TORRID MONTHS OF SPRING, BUT DO NOT ALWAYS PRESAGE LONG-AWAITED RAIN.

Libya, about fifteen years later. And in more recent times, it took only an instant for a sudden downpour to erase a long stretch of the trans-Sahara road that connected In Salah to Tamanrasset, disrupting the entire Arak Gorges region.

The scarcity of rain (always under four inches a year) becomes even more relevant if we consider the desert's thermal potential. Along with the wind, the sun is one of the leading causes of the brutal Sahara climate. Plants, animals, and people must face extremely high temperatures and deal with the problem of constant dehydration: in the summer, peaks of over 120°F are normal, at least below elevations of 3,000 feet. In terms of heat, 133°F in Timimoun, Algeria, and over 136°F in Azizia, Libya, are world records. Aoulef, also in Algeria, holds the record in duration: in July, the temperature is over 106°F more than ten hours a day. For people who live in the Sahara, the ground temperature is much more important. The ground's reflecting power in the Sahara (known as albedo) is extremely high. As the earth is bare and generally light-colored, reflected irradiation can be up to three quarters of the energy received from the sun. In the noonday heat, the air seems to vibrate and the horizon becomes a confused, wavering line. Enormous lakes appear in the distance, sparkling under the sun and reflecting dunes and mountains in a perfectly symmetrical pattern. Mirages, the pièce de résistance of the Sahara's romantic imagination, have a logical explanation that involves the laws of refraction. The layers of hot air at ground level act like a mirror, reflecting objects located on the horizon. The phantom waters of the Sahara are simply refracted images of the sky. But the desert is not always hot: because the Sahara is exceptionally continental, there are extreme fluctuations in temperature between day and night, with differences of 60 degrees in both summer and winter. During the winter, the nights are bitter cold and the thermometer can drop to well below freezing. In the Hoggar, at an elevation of 4,300 feet (at Tamanrasset), the temperature has reached 7°F. These extreme fluctuations are debilitating to the human body, and it is no coincidence that Sahara nomads often suffer from pulmonary ailments. Yet despite the severity of climate conditions, the Sahara has more admirers that it would seem to deserve.

76 The dead city of Djado, at the foot of a plain, stood on the road that connected the Libyan oases with the Lake Chad region, passing the Kawar oases and salt flats.

76–77 The ramparts of other ruined castles seem to rise up near Djado, in the northeast Teneré in Niger: perhaps the city's builders were inspired by the form of such rocks.

78–79 Rare acacias and shrubs dot the deserts of Mauritania, ceaselessly battered by the wind. The Sahara runs all the way to the coast here, meeting the Atlantic directly. Only in the south, along the Senegal River, is subsistence agriculture possible.

80–81 AND 81 MANY OF THE HUNDREDS OF LITTLE ISLETS THAT DOT THE MIDDLE COURSE OF THE NIGER RIVER ARE INHABITED BY FARMERS AND FISHERMEN, DESCENDANTS OF THE FOUNDERS OF THE ANCIENT KINGDOMS WHOSE FORTUNE WAS BASED ON TRANS-SAHARA TRADE. IN ITS GREAT BEND TO THE NORTH, THE NIGER PENETRATES FAR INTO THE DESERT, TRACING THE BORDER BETWEEN THE WORLD OF THE NOMADS AND THAT OF SEDENTARY FARMERS. IN PREHISTORIC TIMES, THE RIVER FLOWED NORTH, FLOODING WHAT IS NOW THE DRY BED OF ARAOUANE, IN MALI.

82–83 FRINGED BY PALMS AND AQUATIC PLANTS, THE FRESHWATER LAKE BOKOU, WHICH IS FOUND AMONG OTHER SALT LAKES AT OUNIANGA SERIR IN CHAD, EVOKES IMAGES OF PARADISE. BUT THIS EDEN IS BESIEGED BY THE EMPTY DESERT.

83 RIGHT THE SAHARA'S SURFACE WATERS ARE ALMOST ALWAYS TOO SALTY TO BE DRINKABLE AND VITAL. THE SALT CONCENTRATION CAN BE SO HIGH THAT THE SHORES BECOME COVERED WITH A THICK CRUST, AS IN THIS LAKE IN OUNIANGA SERIR (TOP), OR IN LAKE YOA NEAR OUNIANGA KEBIR (BOTTOM), WHICH RIVALS THE DEAD SEA IN MINERAL CONTENT.

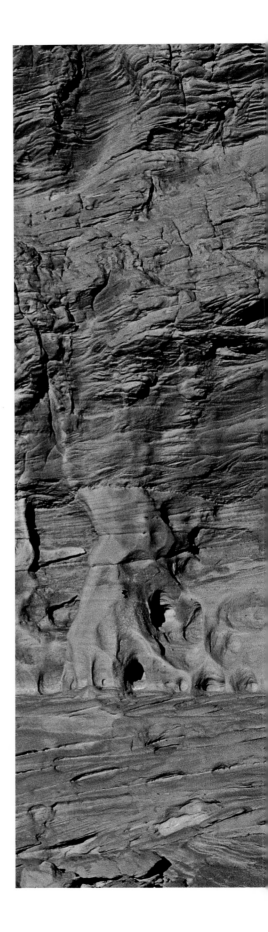

84 TOP A COMPLETELY LIMPID SKY OVER THE LOW ACACUS MOUNTAINS. THE REGION CAN GO FOR YEARS AND YEARS WITHOUT EVER RECEIVING A DROP OF RAIN, BUT DOWNPOURS CAN BE SUDDEN AND SOMETIMES DISASTROUS: IN 1939, MURZUCH WAS COMPLETELY DESTROYED BY AN EXCEPTIONALLY VIOLENT CLOUDBURST.

84 BOTTOM AND 84–85 IN THE LIBYAN REGION OF FEZZAN, TEMPERATURES CAN REACH 117°F IN THE SUMMER AND GO BELOW FREEZING IN WINTER. THE EXTREMELY DRY AIR MAKES IT POSSIBLE TO SEE THE SMALLEST DETAILS OF THE LANDSCAPE FROM A GREAT DISTANCE, WITH THE VAST EXPANSES OF SAND, KNOWN AS *IDEHAN* (OR *EDEYEN*), AND ROCKY TABLES FURROWED BY PARALLEL ROWS OF DRY RIVERS.

86–87 THIS ROCK IN THE ACACUS SEEMS LIKE THE WORK OF AN ARTIST. THE PATINA THAT OFTEN COVERS ROCKS IN THE SAHARA IS DUE TO THE SALTS LEFT BY EVAPORATION, ESPECIALLY IRON AND MANGANESE OXIDES.

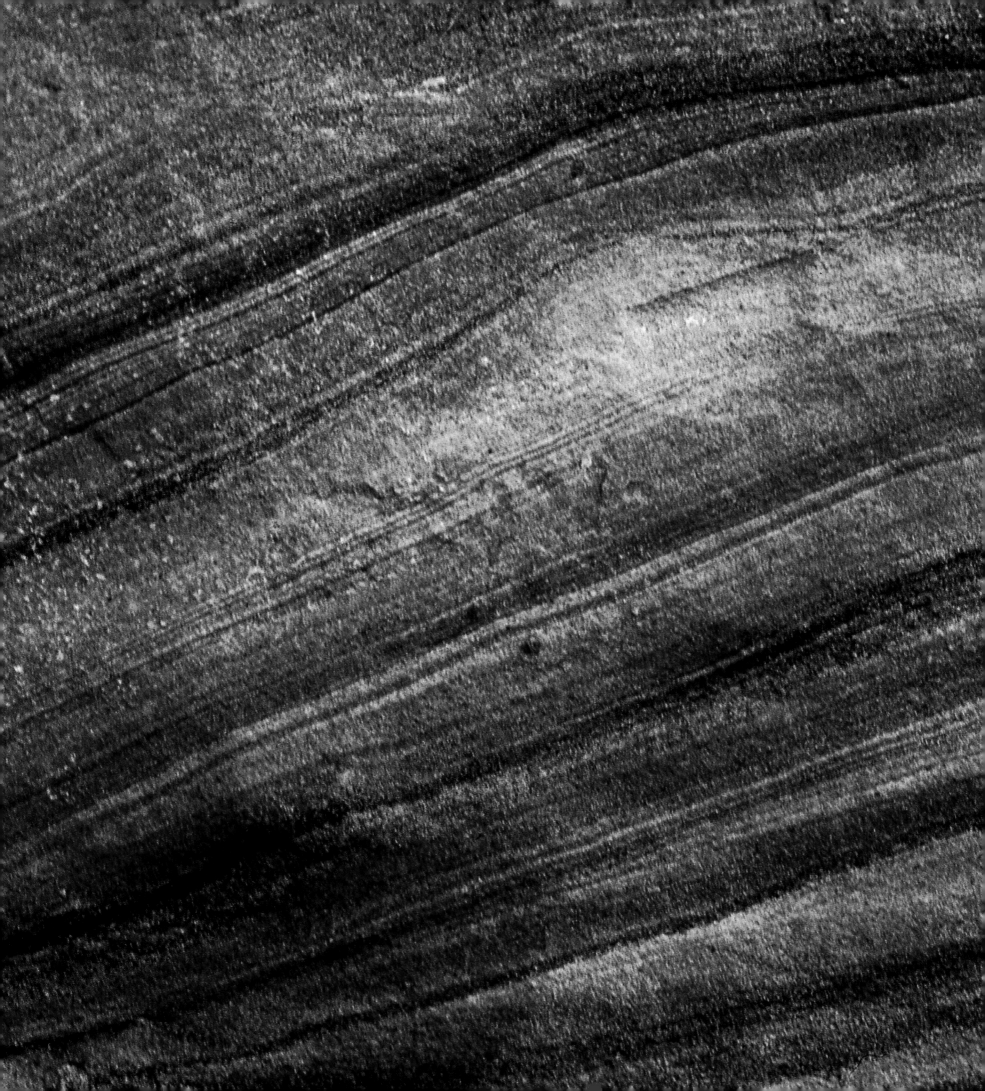

88 AND 89 It is difficult to imagine a fertile past in the mineral desolation of the Acacus. Yet at the start of the Holocene era the climate was subequatorial and the area was populated by all the great mammals of the savanna, as well as humans, who left an invaluable legacy of rock paintings.

90–91 Although the wind constantly shifts the grains of sand, changing the size and appearance of the dunes, the ergs and great isolated dunes of Algeria are essentially stable, and in fact have even become fixed landmarks in the elusive Sahara landscape.

92–93 The siliceous particles that form the dunes and the great accumulations of sand between the Acacus and the Matandous are not produced by the wind, as one might think, but are the result of ancient processes of erosion of the nearby mountains. The sand of the great ergs in fact comes from the Atlas Mountains.

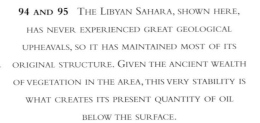

94 AND 95 THE LIBYAN SAHARA, SHOWN HERE,
HAS NEVER EXPERIENCED GREAT GEOLOGICAL
UPHEAVALS, SO IT HAS MAINTAINED MOST OF ITS
ORIGINAL STRUCTURE. GIVEN THE ANCIENT WEALTH
OF VEGETATION IN THE AREA, THIS VERY STABILITY IS
WHAT CREATES ITS PRESENT QUANTITY OF OIL
BELOW THE SURFACE.

96–97 THE MASSES OF DUNES IN THE LIBYAN
DESERT, SOME OF WHICH COVER A SURFACE OF
THOUSANDS OF SQUARE MILES, ARE STILL TODAY A
FORMIDABLE OBSTACLE TO OVERCOME, NOT ONLY
ON CAMELBACK BUT EVEN IN THE MOST POWERFUL
FOUR-WHEEL-DRIVE VEHICLES.

98–99 THE SHEER WALLS OF
TADRART ACACUS SOAR UP TO THE
DEEP BLUE DESERT SKY. THE
MORPHOLOGY OF THE ACACUS IS
QUITE SIMILAR TO THAT OF THE
NEARBY TASSILI N'AJJER IN ALGERIA.
THE WESTERN SIDE OF THE MASSIF
NEAR THE GHAT OASIS IS A
STEEP ESCARPMENT.

100–101 BEHIND THE FINAL CRESTS
OF A GREAT PYRAMID-SHAPED DUNE IN
THE LIBYAN DESERT NEAR GHAT, THE
SCATTERED REMAINS OF A TABULAR
PLATEAU FILL THE HORIZON AS FAR AS
THE EYE CAN SEE. ROCKS, IN THE
FORM OF GRAY AND BROWN RAMPARTS
BROKEN INTO SUN-BLACKENED
SHARDS, PLATES, MASSES, AND SPIRES
DOMINATE THE MORPHOLOGY
OF THE SAHARA.

102–103 THE FORM OF MANY
YARDANGS IN THE "WHITE DESERT" OF
EGYPT ARE SHAPED BY THE WIND INTO
A FORM THAT VAGUELY RESEMBLES A
CROUCHING ANIMAL.

104 Over the course of the millennia, erosion caused by now vanished rivers, the wind, and extreme fluctuations in temperature have crumbled the structure of the Ennedi plateau, shaping these sandstone pinnacles bleached by the sun.

105 TOP LEFT The Tibesti Mountains, parts of which are completely devoid of vegetation, create an uneasy feeling of emptiness. Yet the flora of this massif, where species of Sahel origin predominate, is inexplicably richer than that of the Hoggar.

SECRETS
OF THE MOUNTAINS

About two million years ago, the Sahara massifs were disrupted by a series of extraordinarily powerful volcanic eruptions. Enormous quantities of lava were spewed to the surface, submerging the rocks below and invading the valleys. At the end of the eruptive phase, the forces of erosion went into action, crumbling the walls of the volcanoes and revealing their internal vents, made of solid basalt. The peaks and compact monoliths that characterize Sahara mountain landscapes originated in this process of rapid solidification of lava. While the peaks of the Hoggar and Tibesti Mountains offer an anthology of primal phenomena, the sedimentary formations of Tassili n'Ajjer clearly evidence the role of exogenous agents. The wind, the sun, and especially the corrosive action of now vanished rivers transformed what was once a compact plateau of sandstone into a jungle of canyons, rock columns, towers, and jagged ridges. The legacy of constantly alternating moist and dry periods is plainly evident here. Of the mountains of the central Sahara, the Hoggar massif is indubitably the best known and most important, the true back-

bone of the desert. In its center is a great mountain cap, Atakor, isolated by a moat of flat deserts and surrounded by a series of low massifs lost in the vast plain. For geological, ecological, and human reasons, that great slice of the Sahara between 19 and 27 degrees of latitude north and 1 and 8 degrees of longitude is considered part of the Hoggar. It is a polygon cut in half by the Tropic of Cancer. Its confines are marked by the plains of Tidikelt to the north and by Tanezrouft and Teneré, absolutely flat deserts, to the southeast and west. The Hoggar is a world apart and has always played a special role in the Sahara: from time to time, during various epochs in history, it has acted as a hinge for traffic between Mediterranean Algeria and black Africa, or as a difficult obstacle to overcome. During the military conquest of the Sahara, the so-called pacification of the Hoggar cost the French army dearly: Atakor remained an inviolable fortress for decades. In effect, the entire Hoggar looks like a natural fortress. Atakor, like a turreted castle, extends north in a long ridge called Teffedest, which culminates in the peak of Garet el Djenoun,

105 TOP RIGHT Deeply eroded sandstone towers rise on the plain not far from the Archei gorge, revealing the ancient origins of the Ennedi plateau. The average altitude of the massif is about 3,000 feet.

105 BOTTOM The bizarre rocky formation of the Hoggar reflects the complex geological events that have affected the mountains of the Sahara, which were subject to violent volcanic activity about 2 million years ago.

or the Mountain of Demons (7,733 feet). Around it is a crown of outer bastions: Tassili n'Ajjer, Mouydir, Ahnet, the Tim Missao, Tin Reroh, and Hoggar *tassilis,* and Adrar n Iforhas. Like a solitary outpost, the Tel-ertheba massif stands isolated in a great *reg,* dotted with small volcanic cones that have been consumed over the millennia. Rising up 6,500 feet, it dominates the track that connects Tamanrasset to Djanet, a precious landmark for the caravans returning from the salt mines of Tisemt in the parched plains of Amadror. Teneré begins south of the Amadror basin. It is traversed by the fossil beds of Wadi Tafasasset and Wadi Tin Tarabin, which collect the scarce rainwater from the southeast Hoggar.

nomads makes Tahat and Ilamane protagonists in an epic amorous duel that involves at least two female mountains. So the clear notches carved into the walls of Ilamane are the result of lance and saber wounds; the craters are the imprints the mountains left during titanic duels; and the springs are old wounds that have not yet healed. In the same manner, according to the Tuareg, all natural manifestations, except for mirages, are the work of djinn, desert spirits who are responsible for landslides, whirlwinds, fires, and, of course, echoes. Nothing happens by chance in the Hoggar, a place of hallucinations and waking dreams. The peaks of Atakor are separated by steep valleys, a network of dry torrents

that only rarely come to life after heavy rain. During the winter and spring, the sky over the Hoggar is sometimes covered with clouds, but precipitation is rare. Despite this, at least in the center of the massif, watering holes are relatively frequent. These are for the most part underground springs located along the dry beds of the wadis, at a depth varying from eight inches to fifty feet. When the

Atakor, the central node of this endless complex, is certainly one of the most evocative places in the entire Sahara. Only here can one fully comprehend the extent of the disruption that formed the Sahara mountains. The basalt spires that boldly rise up toward the sky are suddenly succeeded by vast rocky tables, the remains of immense lava flows, in a supernatural chaos. The Tahat and Ilamane, which are almost 10,000 feet high, are the most spectacular features of this landscape. From Assekrem Pass we can clearly distinguish the volcanic nature of the various peaks, of which Ilamane is an exemplary prototype. Surrounded by a wilderness of sawtooth spurs, Ilamane is a favorite subject in Tuareg mythology. The poetic and warrior spirit of the desert

water table is especially high, the water collects in rocky basins known as *gueltas,* little ponds populated by fish and surrounded by luxuriant vegetation. True springs in the Atakor are very rare and can be counted on one hand. The slopes of the massif stretch out for about sixty miles, fading into a ray of plateaus interrupted by flat expanses of pebbles or sand. In this area, the wadis are still living and the presence of water, appropriately channeled, permits stable agricultural settlements. The oases of Tazrouk, Idelès, Hirafok, and Mertoutek, to name just a few, look like actual gardens: citrus fruits, millet, wheat, tomatoes, and every sort of vegetable are grown here, in addition to the ever-present date palm. The situation in the deserts that surround Atakor is quite a dif-

ferent matter. Here, water holes are rare and quite distant from each other. In Tanezrouft, to find the first water hole one must travel to the Tim Missao Tassili, a low plateau suffocated by scorching earth, 125 miles from the nearest oasis. Hoggar Tassili and Tin Reroh Tassili, still little known even today, create the same sensation of abandonment. To the north, the Ahnet massif is, if possible, even more remote and arid: its sandstone rocks rise from the plain like ruined walls. Mouydir and especially Tassili n'Ajjer have wider valleys and more vegetation. The few three-thousand-year-old cypress trees that have survived in the more protected valleys are living testimony of a once milder climate. The oleanders and olives on the banks of some of the gueltas in Atakor also originated in southern Europe. The origins of the two massifs is identical, but eruptive activities were more violent and prolonged in the Tibesti. In certain points, the unusually abundant lava flows were 4,000 feet thick: many table plateaus (here known as *tarsos*), littered with debris and dotted with the remains of ancient craters, were formed entirely by these effusions. In many areas, secondary volcanic activity still occurs, as we can see in the hot mineral springs in the Soborom basin near Bardai, and the fumaroles that can be found as we climb the slopes of Toussidé Peak (10,712 feet). Right at the foot of Toussidé is one of the most surprising phenomena of the Sahara, the so-called Trou au Natron. It is an immense circular crater that is 3.7 miles in diameter and 2,300 feet deep. The bottom of this enormous basin, delimited by sheer black basalt walls, is partially covered by a crystalline layer of pure white sodium carbonate, from which small volcanic cones emerge. Trou au Natron is one of the few places on Earth that can truly be described as appalling. Yet all it takes is one slightly more abundant rainfall than usual to cover the edges of the crater with grasses and colorful flowers, transforming the landscape. This softness is ephemeral and uncommon, as the Tibesti is always arid: useful rain comes in ten-year intervals, and temperatures can fluctuate tremendously. As in the Hoggar, water reserves are concentrated along dry rivers (known as *enneris*), in gueltas, and in the very rare springs. In all,

the inhabitants of the Tibesti can count on about a hundred permanent watering holes, which determine their movements from pasture to pasture and mark their daily existence. One hundred hopes for survival for the people and animals scattered across a territory almost 40,000 square miles in size: the figure adequately explains the famous frugality of the Teda (and their supposed viciousness). The massif is located almost entirely within Chad and could be enclosed within a triangle whose sides are about 250 miles long. The southern summit is marked by mighty Emi Koussi, which at 11,204 feet truly merits the title of roof of the Sahara. To the south, the massif gently slopes down to the edges of the Chad basin. To the north, the slope is instead steep and fractured into thousands of blocks in the most bizarre shapes, the remains of an ancient table plateau: these are the famous Aiguelles de Sissé, which emerge from the plain like a stone archipelago. In the expanse of desert that surrounds the Tibesti, vegetation is almost nonexistent. But the situation improves significantly in the mountains near the gueltas and at the edges of the *enneris*. Of the four hundred species that constitute the flora of the Tibesti, in addition to the ever-present cover of weeds and thorny bushes, there are seven varieties of acacias, jujubes, a few figs, and a quantity of Sahel plants. Tall trees disappear over 6,000 feet in altitude: the rock fields of the *tarso* are practically barren. Given the extreme aridity, fauna is also scarce. Apart from the mouflon, which predominates in the hunting scenes depicted in rock paintings, large mammals are rare: a few gazelles, baboons, jackals, wildcats, and few other species worthy of note. Small rodents and reptiles are more numerous. Little is known of the famous Sahara crocodiles that supposedly live in certain gueltas. Northwest of Chad, near the Sudanese border, there is another large mountain range, the Ennedi, which covers 23,000 square miles. It is an ancient plateau of sedimentary origins whose position has not been disturbed by any significant volcanic activity. Its maximum elevation is only 4,757 feet. The eastern area has absolutely no water and is uninhabited. To Bideyat nomads, it is the Land of Thirst and wandering spirits. The remainder of the massif is less arid, although it receives an average of only 3.5 inches of rain a year. The relative livability of the Ennedi is due to its geographical position, the form and direction of its valleys, and the abundance of groundwater, which guarantees permanent water reserves. Ennedi is what geographers call an ecotone, a special transition area between a super-arid environment and a savanna. The presence of cramcram *(Cenchrus biflorus),* a typical Sahel species, shows that the Ennedi enjoys unusual climate conditions for the Sahara. While plant cover is sparse, it mitigates the effects of evaporation and transpiration of the soil, permitting decent living conditions and providing sufficient pasture for domestic animals. The plateau is connected to Bahr el Ghazal, a great river artery flowing out of Lake Chad. The river is now completely dry, but in the past, even during recent historic times, it experienced significant flooding that carried large amounts of water to the massif. An increase of more than 900 feet in the level

of Lake Chad, due to tectonic movements, seems to have been sufficient to rescue the Ennedi from the desert's clutches. The crocodiles of the Guelta of Archei, which ends in steep red sandstone walls, is a reminder that the connection between Lake Chad and the Ennedi is not just a fantasy, but actually existed and continued for some time. Due to its less harsh climate, fauna in the Ennedi is much more numerous and varied than in the Tibesti. In addition to typical Sahara animals, the area has (or had) savanna species. In the early 1960s there were still cheetahs, African hunting dogs, hyenas, and even lions; giraffes walked up the dry riverbeds well beyond the 16th parallel. Remote and not easily accessible, the Ennedi still has much to reveal to science.

The inventory of Sahara mountains would not be complete without the Air Mountains in Niger and the Sahara Atlas range that runs from Algeria west to southern Morocco. The Air range also follows the common rule in the formation of Sahara mountains: a crys-

talline base with a succession of sedimentary and volcanic activity. This massif, a sort of fossil watershed between the Chad and Niger basins, extends 250 miles north of Agadez, to the Algerian frontier. The Air has a relatively asymmetrical structure: to the west is a great undulating expanse whose hills are no more than 2,625 feet high, furrowed by a parallel series of dry rivers, ancient tributaries of the Azaouak; to the west, looking out over the barren expanse of the Teneré, there are actual mountains that reach their maximum height in the Bagzane Mountains (6,634 feet). Along with Sahara and Sahel vegetation, the Air also has examples of residual flora from temperate zones. Their presence is even more amazing if we consider the distance that separates northern Niger from the Mediterranean Sea. At the far north of the massif, not far from the peak of Mount Gréboun, grow olive trees *(Olea laperrini)* that are between three and four thousand years old. Looking like an engraving by Gustave Doré, the contorted, scaly trunks of these trees are up to eight feet in diameter. Date and doum palms *(Hyphaene thebaica)* grow along the valleys *(koris)* and in the oases. The northwest fringe of the Air is part of the Integral Reserve of the Teneré, proclaimed in 1988 to protect various animal species in danger of extinction: the cheetah, the striped hyena, the caracal, and above all the addax antelope. The Sahara Atlas is the only true mountain range in the great desert: like an immense barrier formed of parallel, broken creases, it cuts Algeria in half for 750 miles from east to west. Its formation is related to alpine orogenesis, which died out here when it encountered the crystalline Sahara shield. The mountains of southern Morocco are the natural extension of this system. The eroded, crumbling rocks of the Sahara Atlas loom over the endless solitude of the desert, tracing the boundary between two different, opposing lifestyles: nomadic and sedentary.

110 SUNSET TINGES THE SANDSTONE PINNACLES OF THE TIBESTI WITH RED AND ORANGE. AT THE FOOT OF THE MOUNTAINS ARE MASSES OF SAND BLOWN BY THE WIND FROM LIBYA. THE REGION, TORMENTED BY WAR AND BORDER DISPUTES FOR DECADES, IS STILL TODAY ONE OF THE MOST INACCESSIBLE REGIONS OF THE SAHARA.

110–111 THE NORTHERN AND WESTERN SLOPES OF THE TIBESTI ARE EVEN HARSHER AND MORE DRAMATIC, CONSISTING OF THE FRACTURED, ERODED REMAINS OF THE PLATEAU, EMERGING LIKE ISOLATED RAMPARTS IN THE PLAIN. THE LANDSCAPE BECOMES ESPECIALLY SPECTACULAR NEAR THE LIBYAN BORDER.

112–113 It is not uncommon to see vestiges of Mediterranean flora, such as olives, oleanders, and cypresses, in the deep valleys that furrow the mountains and plateaus of the Sahara. The most remarkable example is the famous cypresses of Tamrit in the Tassili n'Ajjer, "living fossils" that are three thousand years old.

114–115 This nomadic shepherd of the Ennedi plateau moves slowly toward camp with his dromedaries, following the tree-lined bed of a dried-up river. There is a relative wealth of flora in the region, making the Ennedi an ecotone, a distinct step in the transition between desert and savanna.

116–117 The Archei gorge near Fada, the most important city in the Ennedi region, is a permanent source of water that is extremely important to the nomadic herders in the area, who bring their livestock here to drink. The waters of the guelta are home to a number of crocodiles, testifying to the Ennedi region's past connection with Lake Chad.

118 Wild plants (top) supplement the diet of nomads, which is low in fiber and carbohydrates. Although scarce, Sahara plants have managed to colonize even the most sterile regions like dunes (bottom).

119 Sahara plant species, which concentrate around the few water holes or dried riverbeds, are 60 percent trees and shrubs; the remainder are grasses and legumes.

THE ART
OF SURVIVAL

The response of Sahara dwellers to the harsh living conditions due to lack of water has produced significant changes in their life cycles. Animals can take refuge in underground dens, migrate, or in any event modulate their lives so they can avoid the great daytime heat. For plants, forced to submit fully to the ravages of the climate, life is more complicated: the entire Sahara contains no more than about a thousand plant species, a mere nothing, considering that only 4,000 square miles in equatorial regions could contain three to four thousand species.

Sahara plants face many kinds of hard problems, and must thus adapt to them and develop the expedients necessary to overcome them. Many species can germinate, flower, and die in just one day, taking advantage of unexpected rain. All together they form a carpet of colorful, ephemeral vegetation that suddenly changes the face of the desert and is called *acheb* by Sahara nomads. This frenetic growth activity has a precise purpose: to produce seeds, if possible more than necessary, that can remain dormant for many years, unmindful of the merciless desert sun. The rain may be too brief and fool the biological clock of the seeds, or the wind could suddenly rise to dry out the young seedling. In the absence of alternate strategies, the species would be destined for extinction. But even under optimum conditions some seeds remain inactive, waiting to take advantage of the next favorable cycle. Other plants prefer to trust their seeds to the wind. *Citrullus colocynthis* is a curcurbit that takes root all over the sandy surface of the desert, creating perfectly round fruits that resemble small melons that, once mature, fall off the plant and dry up, becoming extremely light. The wind propels them, making them roll like billiard balls across the flat Sahara plains. In this way, the seeds scatter everywhere, ensuring the survival of the species. The cramcram, a minor flagellum of the Sahara, prefers to use slower but safer means of locomotion. Its seeds are enclosed in a sheath spiked with sharp, treacherous spines that seemed designed specially to catch onto the fur of animals and clothes of humans. No wandering herder is without a set of tweezers in various styles and sizes: they are indispensable for removing the cursed cramcram thorns and inadvertently disseminating them everywhere. Plants in the *Anastatica* genus, like the Rose of Jericho, are highly skilled in using the wind to their advantage. Once it reaches maturity, *Anastatica* dries up and folds in on itself, forming a ball. Its fragile roots then lose their ability to hold the plant to the ground, and the Rose of Jericho becomes easy prey to the strong Sahara winds, which uproot it and carry it away. End of story? No, the plant only fakes its death. In the evening, when the wind calms, *Anastatica* (from the Greek *anàstasis*, "resurrection") comes back to life: taking advantage of the nighttime humidity, the little branches extend, the fruits regenerate, open, and allow their seeds to spill out to create a new colony. The next day, gone with the wind again. At the other extreme, plants that choose to make the best use of their meager underground water resources need to have roots that are as deep and extensive as possible. Certain acacias, like *Acacia nilotica* and *A. raddiana*, push their underground tentacles many yards deep. Some dune grasses, like *Danthonia* and *Aristida pungens,* also have very long but shallow roots that can take advantage of nighttime condensation and occasional rainfall. In the Sahara, competition among living organisms is often ruthless. The space that one often observes between one plant and another is far from accidental.

120-121 The round fruit of *Citrullus colocynthis* creates unexpected spots of color in the arid Sahara plains. Like tentacles, the branches of this plant, covered with hardy foliage, extend out for several feet across the surface of the soil in order to capture as much nighttime humidity as possible.

121 Unlike other living beings, plants cannot take shelter from the wind and sun, nor can they migrate during times of drought. The often wide empty space between one plant and another signals the need to take full advantage of scarce water resources, to the detriment of competitors.

122 ONE CHARACTERISTIC OF MANY XEROPHYTES (FROM THE GREEK *XEROS*, OR "ARID," DENOTING PLANTS THAT LIVE IN DESERT ENVIRONMENTS) IS THE TRANSFORMATION OF LEAVES INTO THORNS. WOODINESS REDUCES TRANSPIRATION, MAKING IT POSSIBLE TO SAVE PRECIOUS RESOURCES. THORNS ARE ALSO AN EFFECTIVE DEFENSE AGAINST PREDATORS.

122–123 A SOLITARY PLANT WHOSE SURFACE ROOTS HAVE BEEN BARED BY THE WIND SEEMS TO DEFY THE IMMENSE SOLITUDE OF THE CENTRAL SAHARA WITH ITS GREEN, FLESHY LEAVES. ITS ABILITY TO SURVIVE IN THE DESERT IS BASED ON STRATEGIES OF ADAPTATION DEVELOPED OVER THOUSANDS OF YEARS.

124 BEETLES ARE SOME OF THE FEW LIVING THINGS THAT FREQUENT THE SANDY, ALMOST COMPLETELY STERILE SURFACE EVEN DURING THE DAY. THEIR THICK EXOSKELETON PROTECTS THEM FROM THE MERCILESS SUN AND ALLOWS THEM TO RESIST THE SAHARA'S EXTREME WEATHER CONDITIONS, HELPING THEM TO CONSERVE THE LIQUIDS THEY NEED FOR SURVIVAL.

125 THE FENNEC *(FENNECUS ZERDA)*, THE SO-CALLED DESERT FOX, IS A NOCTURNAL PREDATOR THAT FEEDS ON SMALL MAMMALS, BIRDS, REPTILES, AND, IF NECESSARY, EVEN BEETLES AND SCORPIONS. QUITE SMALL IN SIZE (WEIGHING NO MORE THAN THREE POUNDS), IT CAN GO WITHOUT WATER FOR LONG PERIODS OF TIME.

The roots of certain species produce toxic and antibiotic substances that prevent the seeds of competitors from germinating. Some plants are covered with waxy substances that close their stomas (pores) and prevent evaporation; others transform their leaves into thorns; and some close up to form tight, compact bushes covered by a shield of tough leaves that protect them from the daytime heat. Some species of tamarisks secrete hygroscopic salts that capture nighttime humidity and allow the plant to store enough water for the next day.

The presence of vegetation, even if sparse and scattered, is an essential condition for the survival of animals. However, endemic Sahara species are rare: no sedentary birds and only three of the sixty-five mammal species are endemic (the fennec, the gerbil, and the addax antelope), along with six reptiles and about a dozen insect species.

Insects are some of the organisms best adapted to life in the desert. Tenebrionid beetles, for example, succeed in procuring the little water they need in a manner that is original, to say the least. Positioning themselves head down on the crests of dunes, they expose their backs to the moisture-laden night wind; condensation forms droplets that slide downward to their mouth apparatus. Crickets, large predator ground beetles, scorpions, and fast solifuges (wind scorpions), are all most active at night. Some

species of ants, forced to deal with the outside environment during daytime to procure food, are covered with a silvery fuzz that reflects the sunlight.

There are about forty reptile species in the Sahara. Almost all have scales that make them waterproof and prevent dehydration. Almost all Sahara reptiles are nocturnal and get all the water and nutrition they need from the insects and cold-blooded animals they eat. Some lizards, such as the spiny-tailed lizard, and the skink have diurnal habits instead. The spiny-tailed lizard, up to sixteen inches long, stores food in its large, spiny tail for use during hard times. The

skink, on the other hand, is a perfect dune dweller: its aerodynamic shape and shiny, smooth skin allow it to "swim" under the sand like a fish, as it seeks out small arthropods and beetles, which always take shelter from the baking sun. The velvety carpet of sand, however, can hide less friendly creatures: this is how the horned viper *(Cerastes cerastes)*, half-buried in the sand, avoids the sun and lays its ambush. Its tracks are unmistakable to the expert eye: *Cerastes* moves laterally, leaving a series of distinctive parallel S-shaped tracks. This system of locomotion, which it accomplishes by alternately raising different parts of its body, probably serves to reduce contact with the burning ground as much as possible.

In the desert, those that do not have a den for refuge must move to survive; it thus seems that birds would have an advantage over creatures that crawl or walk. Yet the ninety or so species of birds that live in the Sahara do not have an easy life. Unlike reptiles, they need to drink, and this requires long daily trips in search of water. Many species, such as roadrunners, spend most of their time on the ground, traveling long distances in search of anything edible. All birds suffer from the high daytime temperatures, and their feathers do not always provide adequate protection against temperature extremes. So they are most active during the coolest times of day—dawn and dusk. Namaqua partridges and sand grouses, sometimes incorrectly called desert partridges, can survive in the most arid regions of the Sahara due to an adaptation that has no rival in the bird world: they have a sort of insulating subcutaneous coat that, like an air chamber, allows them to resist the direct rays of the sun. Namaqua partridges and their chicks must drink every day, but drinking places are often very far from their nests. The partridges solve this problem by immersing themselves almost entirely in the water, soaking their breast feathers. The chicks then suck the water out like a sponge whenever they need to drink. For migratory species, the Sahara is

126 TOP AND 127 LEFT THE ADDAX ANTELOPE (LEFT), DECIMATED BY HUNTING, NOW LIVES ONLY IN THE DESERTS OF NIGER AND MAURITANIA. DORCAS GAZELLES (RIGHT), EMBLEMATIC ANIMALS OF THE SAHARA, ARE COMMON IN LIBYA.

126 BOTTOM UNLIKE THE FENNEC, THE GOLDEN JACKAL (*CANIS AUREUS*) MUST DRINK OFTEN AND IS OMNIVOROUS. IT DOES NOT DISDAIN LIVESTOCK THAT HAS DIED DURING TRANSHUMANCES ACROSS THE DESERT.

127 RIGHT THE DESERT MONITOR (*VARANUS GRISEUS*) CAN ADAPT TO THE MOST DIVERSE ENVIRONMENTS, BUT PREFERS DRY RIVERBEDS AND PLACES RICH IN VEGETATION IN GENERAL. THIS NIMBLE AND HARDY DIURNAL CREATURE FEEDS ON REPTILES AND SMALL MAMMALS, WHICH IT CAPTURES WITH UNUSUAL AGILITY.

simply a formidable obstacle to overcome as quickly as possible. Some species of birds can travel 900 miles across it in just three days. But they pay dearly for their long migratory travels. Of the 220 million swallows that reach sub-tropical Africa each year, only one third return to Europe. When crossing the Sahara, the birds lose an average of half their body weight: incapable of flying any longer, they land on the ground, worn out, where they soon die of exhaustion.

Most animals gather around the rare watering holes and gueltas in the mountains. A few specimens of crocodiles still survive in some gueltas of the Ennedi, having miraculously survived the process of desertification. But crocodiles are not the only relics of a wet Sahara past. The waters of the Sahara are also home to many other survivors whose relatives populate many lakes and rivers in tropical Africa: fish, amphibians, crustaceans, mollusks, and insects have developed forms and behaviors designed to handle the problems of a miniaturized environment that is at constant risk of drought. Some fish, like the genus *Clarias*, can remain buried in the mud for weeks or months. Their physiological features are truly unique. In addition to the normal gill system, *Clarias* have an additional spongy-looking organ that allows them to breath outside of water. If the watering hole where it lives dries up, the versatile *Clarias* takes advantage of the cool night and effortlessly leaves the water to crawl across the sand until it finds a new pool to its liking. Mammals can count on even more sophisticated mechanisms. The jerboa and kangaroo rat are active primarily after sunset, while during the day they hide in their cool dens, where the level of humidity is always constant. The fennec (*Fennecus zerda*), the little desert fox, has enormous ears that are not only per-

fect sensors useful for hunting, but also serve to disperse heat. The desert gazelle (*Gazella dorcas*), and above all the large addax antelopes (*Addax nasomaculatus*), can live for indefinite periods without drinking. How? The explanation is both simple and mind-boggling. Every living being must eliminate water to avoid absorbing heat; however, if the liquids lost are not quickly replaced, an organism will rapidly dehydrate and die. The addax's body reacts in just the opposite way: instead of losing water to cool off, it counterattacks by increasing its body temperature and thus allowing itself to disperse heat. Not only that, but the addax has no problems in handling temperatures over 110°F, which are fatal for the nerve cells of any mammal. While the animal breathes, the blood circulating in the veins of its nostrils cools off and exchanges heat with the arterial flow heading to its brain, which in this way maintains a lower temperature than the rest of its body. Today, the addax is an endangered species, and survives only in the most inaccessible areas of the Sahara, where humans rarely set foot. In 1988, by official decree of the government of Niger, the Addax Sanctuary was established in the Teneré. It is an integral reserve where the presence of humans and vehicles is strictly limited. Not only the addax lives in this enormous expanse of almost 30,000 square miles; other endangered species, like the cheetah and the striped hyena inhabit this area. The reserve is not only intended to protect animals, but also to rationalize the use of the region's natural resources and improve the living conditions of the nomads. So the Teneré itself, a desert within deserts, opens to a vision of the Sahara as a place for life and a school of adaptation, a global ecosystem awaiting a new equilibrium.

128 AND 129 THE SAND CAT FEEDS PRIMARILY ON BIRDS, LIZARDS, INSECTS, AND SMALL MAMMALS. BUT ITS EXTRAORDINARY AGILITY MAKES IT A MATCH FOR MORE DANGEROUS ANIMALS, LIKE THIS HORNED VIPER, WHOSE BITE COULD BE FATAL.

130 AND 131 WITH RAPID UNDULATING MOVEMENTS, A HORNED VIPER BURIES ITSELF IN THE SAND, ALLOWING ONLY ITS EYES AND THE TOP OF ITS HEAD TO EMERGE.

132–133 A SKILLED, RUTHLESS HUNTER, THE CARACAL, ALSO KNOWN AS THE DESERT LYNX (*CARACAL CARACAL*), CAN REACH FORTY POUNDS IN WEIGHT.

133 EQUIPPED WITH EYES MADE FOR NIGHT VISION, A DUNE GECKO (*STENODACTYLUS PETRII*) SCRUTINIZES THE AREA IN SEARCH OF INSECTS AND ARACHNIDS.

PROGENY OF THE SUN

134 AND 135   THE FACES OF SAHARA PEOPLES EXPRESS THE DEPTH OF TRADITIONS AND CULTURES FORGED OVER THOUSANDS OF YEARS OF HARD LIFE IN THE DESERT.

136   THE ALIGNMENT OF THESE ROCKS IN ERG UAN KASA, IN THE LIBYAN FEZZAN, IS ONE OF THE MYSTERIES OF THE SAHARA: PERHAPS IT IS A NEOLITHIC NECROPOLIS.

137   THE INCESSANT MOVEMENT OF SAND OFTEN REVEALS MYSTERIOUS VESTIGES FROM THE PAST: PRE-ISLAMIC TOMBS LIKE THIS ONE SOUTH OF DJANET, ALGERIA (LEFT), LITHIC TOOLS PHOTOGRAPHED IN THE EGYPTIAN DESERT (CENTER), OR NEOLITHIC GRINDSTONES THAT EMERGE FROM THE BARE SOIL OF THE TENERÉ IN NIGER (RIGHT).

THE FIRST INHABITANTS OF THE SAHARA

The desert has not always been uninhabited. Traces of vanished civilizations that flourished when the Sahara was still green emerge from the shadowy past. The gradual advance of drought that began about five thousand years ago was what pushed ancient Sahara dwellers to take refuge in the mountains, where life was still possible. There, in an enormous open-air museum, obscure artist-shamans left thousands of paintings and graffiti on the sandstone walls: masked dancers, epic scenes of elephant and buffalo hunts, and graceful profiles of spotted cattle. Then the Sahara became a place where human beings were biological losers and nomadism became an absolute necessity. Current desert peoples, nomadic herders of dromedaries, cows, and goats, are the latest heroes in this thousand-year-old epic.

The drying up of water and consequent disappearance of plants and animals over the various epochs directly influenced the population of West Africa. Unfortunately, with the exception of the Neolithic period, it is not easy to date these migratory movements. One thing for certain is that for the past 2 million years, from the early Pleistocene on, human beings have never completely abandoned the Sahara. This is demonstrated by the abundance of lithic discoveries scattered all across the desert. The first worked stones, discovered in Algeria, date back a million and a half years. Unfortunately, the identity of their creators is unknown, as human fossils from that period are almost completely absent in the Sahara. Later examples of this stone-working technique are more refined, and the rocks show traces of flaking on two sides, preparing the advent of a new type of tool: the elegant and enigmatic bifacial. With the gradual appearance of *Homo sapiens* about sixty thousand years ago, lithic industry tended to miniaturize and become more refined, culminating in the so-called Aterian period (from the name of a region in Algeria). Bifacial tools were gradually replaced by a more specialized generation of cutting tools: scrapers, punchers, tanged points, flaked blades, spheroid hammer stones, and chisels. Aterian industry extended across the entire Sahara and is absolutely original in style. The dating for this phase is very controversial, and we should consider it more of a coexistence of styles and different, constantly evolving human groups. The scenario that evokes the Aterian, beginning forty thousand years ago, is a green and irrigated Sahara with a wide variety of flora and fauna. From an opportunistic economy of plundering food and gathering wild fruits, ancient dwellers of the Sahara went on to become hunters, developing new models of social culture. Research conducted on the site of an Aterian

encampment in the Libyan desert shows the vast variety of prey available to hunters: the site has revealed remains of slaughtered rhinoceroses, zebras, gazelles, warthogs, ostriches, tortoises, and various species of birds. And we cannot assume that the mysterious Aterians did not approach a sort of early agriculture, in the form of organized control of useful plants. Aterian culture vanished about twenty thousand years ago, with the advent of an extremely arid period. Driven out by the encroaching desert, Sahara populations gradually retreated to less hostile areas, perhaps the Sahel or northern coastal regions. The arid period persisted until the beginning of the Holocene, about ten thousand years ago. Then the rivers began to flow again, once more filling the lake beds. Plants and animals slowly began to recolonize the Sahara. And they were once again followed by humans.

The population grew at intervals, following various migration routes from the Guinea region, the Nile Valley, and North Africa. We know nothing of these post-Aterian groups or their lifestyle, but such a significant ecological cycle could have spurred them to drastically change well-settled economic and social models. Encountering a favorable environment must have facilitated the change already under way, which finally led to the Neolithic. But it's risky to divide Sahara civilization into a series of evolutionary steps. We should rather imagine a dynamic system comprised of open sociocultural groups in continuous interaction with each other. Herding, hunting, gathering, and preagricultural techniques overlapped and mutually integrated. It is interesting to note that in Africa, these fundamental lifestyles continue to coexist even today. It thus makes sense to imagine a mosaic of different peoples, linked by an ancient common tradition, who developed mixed production systems based on the varied environments. The fact is that in just a few thousand years, there were stable, numerous populations all over the Sahara. By now, these groups had developed an extremely sophisticated lithic technology (microliths), practiced burial rites, and competed for control of resources. The late Stone Age was characterized by different materials than in the past: common cutting stones were cast aside and finer, harder-to-locate materials were preferred, like hyaline quartz, chert, and colored jasper. In producing microliths, regular geometric forms were created that were made to be mounted on wood and bone handles: the compound tool made its first appearance. Use of the bow, so frequently depicted in Sahara rock paintings, probably dates to this period. The time was ripe for what is improperly called the "Neolithic revolution." In reality, rather than a sudden turning point, this was a complex change that varied based on geographical area. We may thus speak of a Teneré Neolithic, a Capsian Neolithic (from the Gafsa oasis in Algeria), a Sudanese Neolithic, and so on, indicating focal points of civilization that had original features yet mutually influenced each other. A domestic art was born during this period that produced clay pots in graceful, finely decorated forms made

for various purposes. Ostrich eggs were worked into disk shapes and holes were drilled into them to produce material for necklaces and ornaments, embellished with bone, ivory, and amazonite beads. New techniques seemed to develop endlessly, expressing themselves in a variety of astounding objects. This incredibly fertile period, which ran roughly from the fifth to the first millennium B.C., was marked by the triumph of herding, which became increasingly important economically. As life became less and less precarious due to the domestication of animals, deep changes occurred in the lives of Sahara dwellers. Communities became more numerous and ownership of livestock, especially cattle, required seasonal movements from pasture to pasture, which translated into a model of life that alternated between a sedentary and nomadic existence. Once basic needs were met, there was also more time to dedicate to abstract thought, ritual, and art. This is demonstrated not only in the thousands of graffiti and lovely stone paintings that make the Sahara an immense open-air museum, but also the numerous examples of statuettes that portray cattle, gazelles, and rams. The constant presence of grindstones and millstones seems to indicate that mineral and vegetable substances were being ground to obtain dyes or medicinal powders, thus leading to body painting and magical/religious practices codified in a set liturgy. The profusion of these objects, associated with shovels and other digging tools, could, however, indicate a much more important fact: that the Sahara was a cradle of agriculture. From about 3,000 B.C., rapidly advancing desertification waylaid any possible developments in this evolution: the exodus of populations to the south and the mountains, where there was still enough water for the herds, was gradual but massive. But it was not a permanent abandonment: the Sahara became a place for seasonal migrations, a passageway, and a trading route. The desert caravan heritage has its roots in this shadowy period, when written history had not yet begun and archaeology struggles to find tools for investigation.

140 THE SPOTS ON THESE ENORMOUS GIRAFFES CARVED INTO THE ROCKS OF THE AIR MOUNTAINS IN NIGER WERE SKILLFULLY DONE WITH GREAT ATTENTION TO DETAIL.

141 TOP LEFT WADI MATHANDOUS IN THE LIBYAN FEZZAN HAS EXCEPTIONAL WORKS OF ROCK ART LIKE THE PROFILE OF THIS EQUID, PERHAPS A WILD ASS.

THE LARGEST
MUSEUM IN THE WORLD

Tens of thousands of graffiti and paintings have been catalogued throughout the immense Sahara, but most of them are concentrated within the great mountains in the center of the desert, where settlements were larger and more lasting: the Hoggar, the Tibesti, the Ennedi, the Air, and the Tassili n'Ajjer–Tadrart Acacus range on the southern borders of Libya and Algeria. Yet favorable climate conditions and material needs are not enough to explain the enormous quantity of sites or their concentration in certain areas. In Jabbaren in Tassili n'Ajjer, in a square 2,000 feet long, there are over five thousand paintings in a wide variety of styles. Like many others, Jabbaren was probably a sacred place, and from this perspective, the Sahara mountains become desert cathedrals, sanctuaries responsible for receiving and transmitting religious and magical rituals. Religious topography in the Sahara, as elsewhere, can be quite precise: images crowd and overlap each other on the site, on one wall only, while nearby surfaces are left bare, even though they would have served quite well for the same purpose.

So who is responsible for the Sahara rock wall paintings and graffiti? Why and what did they paint? The materialistic approach, which sees paintings as representations of reality, does not sufficiently explain this seemingly incomprehensible quantity of subjects and scenes. But there are new theories that seem more promising, even though they are not complete. Perhaps ancient Sahara artists painted what no one saw—that is, what appeared in their heads. In this case, the paintings would be true spiritual metaphors created by ritual specialists, members of residual groups of Bushman-like hunter-gatherers. Recent discoveries of skulls that are anthropometrically similar to the San of the Kalahari lead us to believe that these peoples may once have lived in the Sahara. On the other hand, throughout west and central Africa there is a tradition of small-statured indigenous peoples who preceded settlements

141 TOP RIGHT THIS CARVING SHOWS THE FIGURE OF THE GIANT LONG-HORNED BUFFALO, *BUBALUS ANTIQUUS*, A SYMBOL OF STRENGTH AND POWER

141 BOTTOM GIVEN THE ABSENCE OF ORGANIC FINDS AT THE SITES, THE AGE OF THE CARVINGS AT WADI MATHANDOUS, LIKE THIS BOVID WITH GREAT HORNS, IS QUITE DIFFICULT TO ESTABLISH.

of Bantu and Sudanese groups. The Tellem pygmies who lived in the caves in the Bandiagara fault in present-day Dogon territory, are one example. These painter-shamans, who achieved a trance state using well-tested methods or with the aid of hallucinogenic drugs, believed they had the power to visit the spirit world. Like a caste of priests, they handled relationships with supernatural powers on behalf of nomad shepherds and sedentary early agricultural communities, who lived their lives in the valleys far from sacred places. In

frescoes of this period are reminiscent of the physical effects induced by trance and seem to confirm the shamanic origins of Sahara rock art. Of course, many paintings may be educational or simply an inventory of the outside world, but others require a different interpretation that opens secret doors to the magical and symbolic world. While keeping local variations in mind, we can generally distinguish five artistic cycles characterized by uniform subjects and styles. The first is the so-called Bubalus or large wild animal style: it is certainly the oldest, with its roots in a Paleolithic subsistence economy based on hunting. The predominant animal is in fact *Bubalus antiquus*, a large extinct hartebeest that appeared on the scene at the dawn of the Quaternary period. Along with the hartebeest appear elephants, hippopotamuses, rhinoceroses, giraffes, felines, and all the magnificent animals of Africa. Hunting scenes often show hunters

precolonial times, similar practices were extremely common throughout Africa. The Xhosa of South Africa used the Bushmen as diviners, and the Tutsi of Rwanda still do the same with the pygmies. Even the Samburu herders of Kenya turn to Okiek hunters for their circumcision rites. The belief that falling into a trance profoundly alters perception and frees the body's spirit, makes contact with the supernatural possible, a voyage into the invisible world. The shaman can thus be possessed by the spirit of an animal or a legendary ancestor, taking on their appearance and their power. This supernatural power can be used to heal illnesses, drive away evil spirits, and harmonize the disorder of earthly life with the cosmic order. Identification with a mythical being is often emphasized by masks and headdresses, typical elements of Round Head art. The contracted positions, torsos bent backwards, and flying figures present in many

with beak-shaped heads and zoomorphic shapes tracking or capturing wild animals. Graffiti predominate during this period. Sometimes they are quite large and done on surfaces out in the open. Some figures are gigantic, like the twelve giraffes at Ti-n-Tehad (Wadi Djerat, Tassili n'Ajjer): the largest is twenty-eight feet high. The work of the Bubalus period shows remarkable technical skill: the engraved outline is continuous, and the semicircular groove is usually quite deep and has been smoothed. In certain cases, the animal's body has been hammered with speckles to create the effect of fur or spots. Other carvings depict monstrous creatures, matings with animals and surreal hunts: we see elephants walking on two legs, prodded by a person carrying a stick; in In Habeter, Libya, there is an image of a rhinoceros being captured and dragged by one foot by a dog-headed creature.

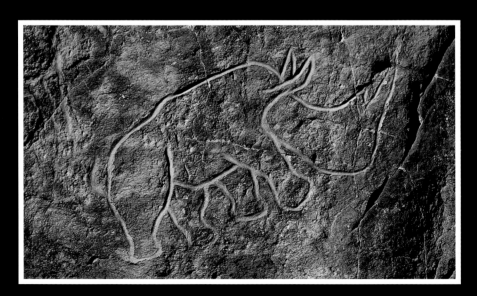

144 FROM THE MAGNIFICENT FIGURES OF AFRICAN WOMEN AT NIOLA DOA IN CHAD (TOP), TO THE GRAFFITI OF BOVIDS AND ELEPHANTS AT WADI MATHANDOUS IN LIBYA (CENTER AND BOTTOM), THESE "ROCK WRITINGS" TELL THE STORY OF THE SAHARA.

145 THE TERARART SITE NEAR DJANET IS KNOWN FOR VARIOUS FIGURES OF BOVIDS THAT SEEM TO BE DRINKING: THE SNOUTS OF THE ANIMALS ARE TURNED TOWARD A DEPRESSION THAT MUST ONCE HAVE BEEN FULL OF WATER.

146–147 GIRAFFES, OFTEN DEPICTED IN HERDS, ARE SOME OF THE MOST COMMON SUBJECTS OF WADI MATHANDOUS GRAFFITI. LOCAL CARVINGS ALSO INCLUDE INSCRIPTIONS IN THE ANCIENT BERBER ALPHABET, TIFINAGH.

The Round Head period is associated with clearly delineated areas of the Sahara: the Tassili-Tadrart and Ennedi ranges. The graffiti technique is for the most part supplanted by painting, which opens the door to new possibilities of expression. The dominant figures in this cycle are vaguely outlined anthropomorphic creatures, with bulges and strange appendices protruding from them. These figures, which are sometimes enormous, have rounded heads with no identifying features. Along with this cast of enigmatic figures, the walls of Tassili and Tadrart are filled with mysterious symbols: simple and double spirals, lines that snake away from subjects and surround them, like a fence or a cocoon, and hand prints on the rock. The most well known example of Round Head art is on a sandstone wall at the Sefar site. The Great God emerges majestically from the center

of a complex of over fifty images done at different times. Ten feet high, his arms are open, almost as if receiving into himself the crowd of praying women, their heads hidden under headdresses as they clap their hands or levitate. In its final phase, the Round Head style changes considerably. The figures of wild animals become smaller and human images are embellished with details: crests and delicate hairstyles gradually replace the spherical helmets. Something seems to be changing, not only in terms of climate: a new socioeconomic order is appearing over the horizon. This is the age of the herders: cows, on which the economic prosperity of the group depended, replace wild animals, becoming the new symbol of power. Images of bovines are extremely detailed, and individual animals can even be distinguished from each other. There are frequent celebratory pictures of daily life: in Iheren, in the northern Tassili, a large herd of sheep occupies the open space among the huts, while the inhabitants of the village attend to their usual affairs. The magical-ritual

element is less evident than in the Round Head period, even though there are the usual levitating figures, mating scenes with masked anthropomorphic creatures, and mysterious figures with bird heads that are clearly reminiscent of ancient Egypt. Beginning in the third millennium, the Sahara underwent its last, permanent cycle of desertification. Rivers and lakes dried up and the desert gradually took over. Pastoral society underwent a crisis, and the exodus of Sahara peoples began as they headed to neighboring regions where the climate was still good for livestock. The horse began to appear in rock art, introduced from Asia to Egypt around 1500 B.C. Horses are almost always shown hitched to two-wheeled chariots, in a position called the "flying gallop." Human figures often appear on the chariots, delineated with a few geometric outlines. The paintings become monochrome, in a brownish red color. We see a slow exhaustion of themes and styles that coincides with the abandonment of the territory by herders and their herds. The Horse period slowly passed away, fading into the mists of time. Next to the pictures appear the first inscriptions in Tifinagh, the ancient Libyan-Berber alphabet. At the start of the Christian era, the horse permanently made way for the dromedary, the only domestic animal capable of surviving in what was now a true desert, arid and uninhabitable. The quality of paintings and carvings further deteriorated, sometimes reduced to a barely sketched outline. The Camel period continued to almost modern times, with no significance other than the human attempt to leave its mark.

PEOPLES
OF THE SAHARA

Present-day populations of the Sahara, about 3 million persons including nomads and the sedentary peoples of the oases, probably descend from the proto-Berber and black races that were prominent during the late Neolithic period. With the start of the last phase of desertification, movements in the various communities scattered throughout the immense territory of the Sahara became frenetic: the rapid deterioration of the environment triggered an impressive number of brief, short-range migrations. The various groups intermingled and divided into tribes and subtribes, confederations, and families whose numbers could change rapidly. There was certainly contact with the Mediterranean world and the Nile Valley. Nomadism became a necessity in this highly mobile scenario of permanent exoduses, returns, and seasonal movements. While farmers gathered in places where water was still abundant and the soil more fertile, herders were left with lands that could not be used for cultivation but had a wealth of natural pastures. Gradually, herders were expelled from villages and scat-

tered throughout the territory. These events from the distant past began to shape the ethnic and philosophical culture of nomadism, which included the cult of individual liberty, austerity, intolerance for laws and restrictions, and an obsessive attachment to livestock. This is true of the Tuareg, the Tebu, and the Mauri tribes of the western Sahara, as it is for the Peul, whose purely Saharan origins are no longer seriously questioned. Classical literature refers to the ancestors of these and other peoples by fantastical names: Nasamones, Gaetulians, Numidians, Atarantes, Ethiopian troglodytes, Augilae. Arab expansion in the Maghreb and the great trans-Saharan trade further complicated the picture, triggering more intermingling and separation. New groups driven by religious zealotry, like the Mzabites, or dedicated to systematic raiding, like the Chaamba Arabs, settled in northern and central Sahara. Even today, the vicissitudes of Sahara peoples are anything but over: new, powerful political and economic forces have had a deep impact on this complex mosaic of cultures and races.

153 TOP A TUAREG CHILD FROM DJANET (LEFT), A YOUNG MAURI WOMAN AND MAN (CENTER AND RIGHT). IN ADDITION TO ETHNIC AFFINITIES, TODAY SAHARA NOMADS ALSO SHARE A GRADUAL SOCIAL MARGINALIZATION.

153 BOTTOM UNLIKE THE MAJORITY OF PASTORAL SOCIETIES, LIVESTOCK HAS NO GREAT CULTURAL SIGNIFICANCE FOR THE MAURI, BUT IS CONSIDERED PRIMARILY AN ECONOMIC ASSET.

155 *TAGILMUST*, DRAPED VEILS THAT COVER THE FACES OF ADULT TUAREG, CAN BE AS MUCH AS FIFTEEN FEET LONG. THE MOST PRIZED ARE DYED WITH NATURAL INDIGO, WHICH COLORS THE SKIN A VERY DESIRABLE BLUISH COLOR. SHOWING ONE'S FACE TO STRANGERS IS CONSIDERED RUDE.

THE BERBERS AND TUAREG

Standing out among the populations of the Sahara is a large group of peoples who are different yet share a close linguistic kinship: the Berbers. The Arabs grouped the white populations of North Africa under this term, passing it down to this day. Berbers include the Sahara and Sahel Tuareg; the mountain people of the Moroccan Atlas and the Algerian Cabili; the Mozabites, inhabitants of the oases of Tuat and Tidikelt in Algeria, and those in Ghadames, Libya; and the Zenaga in Mauritania, to name some of the most important. Of all Sahara peoples, the Tuareg are certainly the best known. The first European explorers of the Sahara were easily seduced by the myth of the "Blue Men," rulers of inaccessible places and ferocious marauders. The habit of concealing their faces behind a veil only increased the aura of mystery that surrounded them. The origins of the Tuareg, long the subject of romantic speculation, are actually much more mundane. From the seventh to the ninth centuries, when waves of Arab invasions pushed out toward North Africa, most Berber tribes accepted the new rulers and the Islamic religion, but some groups refused to submit, instead maintaining their own customs, language, and traditional social organization. The Arabs called these people Tawariq, or "Abandoned by God." The Tawariq, or Tuareg, were forced to retreat to the most remote areas of the Sahara, where the new masters of the land could not find them. Nomadism, based on breeding and using dromedaries as riding and pack animals, became an inevitable choice. In this way, the Tuareg not only succeeded in maintaining their independence, but also managed to control caravan traffic, which in the twelfth century had begun to develop between the Mediterranean and black Africa. In that period, the various tribes, which in the meantime had created a confederation, settled in vast regions of the Sahara, extending their influence to the southern edges of the desert. For centuries, the Tuareg made their fortune by raiding and systematically charging tolls on the caravans that traveled along the endless roads of the Sahara. The arrival of the French suddenly changed the rules of the game: the abolition of slavery and the decline in trans-Sahara trade shook the very roots of traditional society, which was based on a rigid caste system. Subjected by force, the old desert marauders helplessly stood by as their way of life was destroyed. The Tuareg's present territory, which holds about 300,000 people, covers an enormous area, twice the size of western Europe, that includes vast portions of Niger, Mali, Algeria, and Libya.

Tuareg society is divided into *kels* (tribes), which are located in different regions that may be extremely distant from each other: still, kels have the same social organization and speak the same language (Tamashek or Tamahaq). Six large groups can be distinguished, which generally take their name from the area where they live. The Kel Hoggar, or Hoggar Tuareg, occupy the Atakor massif and the broad plains that surround it. The Kel Ajjr live in Tassili n'Ajjer and the adjacent Fadnoun plateau. The Kel

156 THE LANGUAGE THIS MOROCCAN BERBER WOMAN SPEAKS HAS MUCH IN COMMON WITH THE IDIOMS OF MOST PEOPLES IN THE CENTRAL AND WESTERN SAHARA.

157 TOP YOUNG MAURI LIVE IN AN EXTREMELY HIERARCHICAL YET QUITE FLEXIBLE SOCIETY: ABILITY HAS MUCH TO DO WITH IMPROVING ONE'S SOCIAL STATUS.

157 BOTTOM TUAREG WOMEN DO NOT USE THE VEIL AND LOVE TO ACCENTUATE THEIR BEAUTY WITH MAKEUP MADE OF OCHRE POWDER.

158–159 A BERBER MOTHER FROM MOROCCO NURSES HER DAUGHTER AS HER COMPANIONS SHELL ALMONDS. WOMEN ENJOY GREAT AUTONOMY IN THEIR SOCIETY.

Air live in the mountainous area of the Air, in Niger. South of Agadez is the territory of the Kel Gress, an area relatively rich in water and pastures, enough to permit cattle breeding. The Kel Iforhas live in the low mountains of the same name in Mali. The Kel Timbuktu, also known as the River Tuareg, wander along the great bend of the Niger. The extended family is the foundation of the Tuareg social structure. The various families belong to clans, dominated by nobles *(imohar)* at the top, once warriors and now camel herders. The next level below is the vassals *(imrad),* of less pure origins and breeders of the most unworthy sheep. The lowest rank is for farmers of the oases and house servants *(haratin* and *iklan),* dark-skinned descendants of former slaves captured during incursions and raids. Outcast from society, but in reality extremely important and respected, are the *inaden,* versatile smiths and artisans. The *inaden* are also the repositories of oral tradition, and are familiar with extensive genealogies, stories, and arcane secrets. They are often invited to important meetings, and their opinions are heard and respected by all. At the top of the kel system is the *amenokal,* literally "the owner of the land," the supreme authority, elected for life by the nobles. His lineage has legendary foundations and can be traced back to an ancestor mother, the queen Tin Hinan. Descent is matrilineal, while the succession of material goods is generally through the male line. Tuareg women enjoy significant freedom and consideration. They are not required to wear a veil and can not only choose their partner but can also repudiate him when they want without incurring any social sanctions. The Tuareg practice monogamy, and adultery is considered a serious offense. In general, relationships between the sexes are extremely respectful. Girls are valued for their light step, demeanor, and other abstruse qualities like the elasticity of the Achilles tendon, which is believed to indicate virginity. Young people meet during the *ahal,* or arena of love. Ahals can be opportunities for licentious behavior (as the Tuareg put it, the chance "to run unbridled"), but more often it involves modest collective flirting to the sound of the *imzad,* a sort of monotone violin. Women's clothing is rather simple: a long black or dark blue cotton dress that hangs down to the calves, and a shawl of the same color to cover the head. The tall, slender men are much more interested in elegance, wearing wide trousers and mantles to allow movement and permit the circulation of air as a defense against the noonday heat. By age fifteen or sixteen, all adults wear the veil, known as *tagilmoust.* This is a carefully draped strip of cloth that totally hides the face except for the eyes. The veil not only satisfies the vanity of its wearer, but it also protects the skin from the harsh sun, and the indigo dye acts as a protective cream. Covering the face, which makes one both anonymous and terrifying, is also consistent with the mentality of the professional bandit.

Today, the lives of the Tuareg are much quieter than in the past. They seek out new pastures and engage in trade according to the changing seasons, a slow rhythm based on repetitious activities and routes. Pastoral movements follow established cycles, as does care of the herds: grazing, milking, watering, and counting heads. When the day draws to an end and they return to the camp, it's time for tea, a delight and comfort to desert men. To the Tuareg, drinking tea is a ritual. Three cups are served: one for the guest, one for the master of the house, and finally, one for the glory of Allah. The drink, which is very concentrated and strong, contains alkaloids that create a sense of well-being and assuage hunger and thirst. When millet flour and dates have almost run out, sugary tea is often the only nourishment caravan drivers can get.

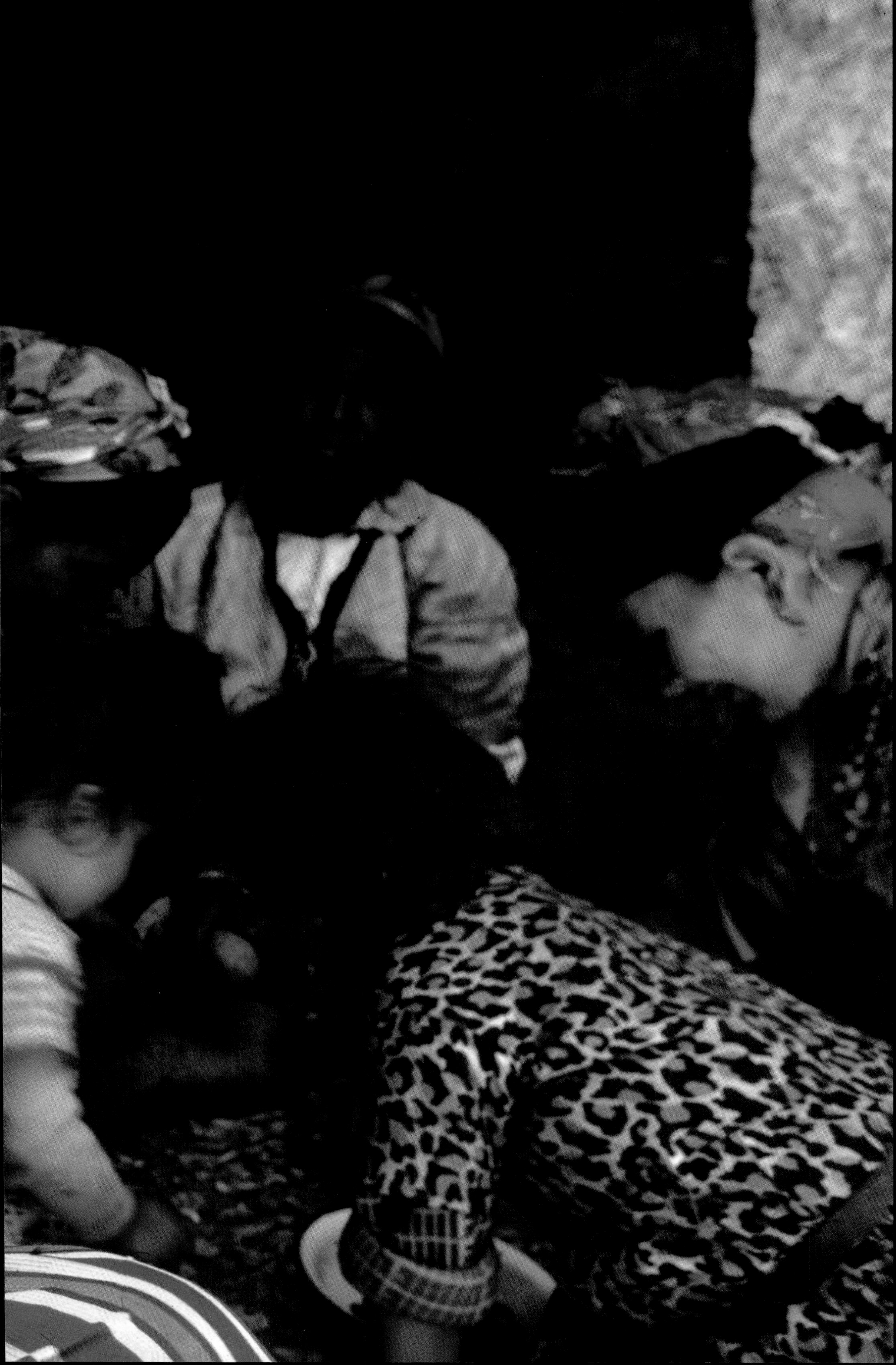

160 IN A STREET IN MARRAKECH'S OLD CITY, A GROUP OF BERBER WOMEN TAKE A BREAK FROM THEIR DAILY ACTIVITIES. ALTHOUGH INFLUENCED BY ARAB CULTURE AND ISLAM, WOMEN IN BERBER CULTURES ARE NOT SEGREGATED.

161 THIS OLD BERBER MAN ENJOYS CONSIDERABLE SOCIAL STANDING WITHIN HIS GROUP. ESPECIALLY IN RURAL AREAS, TRADITIONAL CULTURE HAS REMAINED QUITE VITAL, AND MANY PRE-ISLAMIC CUSTOMS CONTINUE TO THIS DAY.

162–163 A pause for sugary tea flavored with mint leaves interrupts the songs and dances of this Berber folk group, which has come to Marrakech for the spring festival.

163 Berber girls love to adorn themselves with magnificent jewelry during the festival. This girl's headband and necklace are an assembly of silver coins, amber, coral, and glass beads.

164 AND 165 These girls, wearing their best clothes and dressed up in exquisite amber necklaces, are getting ready to pick their future husbands at the September *moussem* (festival) in Imilchil, in the Moroccan Middle Atlas Mountains.

166 AND 167 Nomads' only material possessions are what can be carried by their pack animals. When they break camp, they must bring everything they own with them, including the tent frame (left). For short trips, all they need is a little food, personal belongings, and a supply of water (right).

168–169 Two Tuareg lead their camels, burdened with a precious cargo of salt, in the sandy desert near Timbuktu.

170 These Tuareg from the Air Mountains still engage in barter and traditional trade, but many of their friends and relatives are wage-earners in Arlit and Agadez.

171 The Tuareg do not always bring their tents as they move from pasture to pasture; sometimes all that's needed is a natural shelter against the cold nights. But evening tea is a must.

172 AND 173 THE CLOTHING WORN BY TUAREG
WOMEN IS NOT MUCH DIFFERENT FROM THAT OF
THE MEN. IT CONSISTS OF A LONG TUNIC OPEN
UNDER THE ARMPITS, AND VARIOUS TYPES OF
SHAWLS/HEAD COVERINGS DYED WITH INDIGO.

174 AND 175 ELEGANCE SEEMS A NATURAL
ATTRIBUTE OF THE TUAREG, BOTH WHEN IT IS
ENHANCED BY THE JEWELRY THEY WEAR WHILE
ATTENDING A WEDDING (LEFT), AND IN THE SIMPLE
FORM FAVORED BY THIS ALGERIAN GIRL (RIGHT).

le vélo de ali
ali va à vélo
vite ali vite ali
papa a
pipe
mina sani ali
sani a une
jeudi le 1er décembre
2 - 1 = 1
1 - 1 = 0
1 + 1 = 2
2 - 1 = 1

176–177 Under the vigilant eye of his teacher, a child learns the rudiments of French in a school for nomads in Niger. Although education is fundamental for survival in modern society, governments have often used educational requirements to force nomads to become sedentary.

178 AND 179 TUAREG FESTIVALS LIKE THIS CELEBRATION IN IN GALL, NIGER, ARE ALWAYS QUITE COLORFUL. SUMPTUOUSLY DRESSED MEN DANCE WITHIN A CIRCLE OF WOMEN TO THE OBSESSIVE BEAT OF TAMBOURINES. SONGS, SOMETIMES IMPROVISED, EVOKE THE LEGENDARY EXPLOITS OF ILLUSTRIOUS PERSONS AND DAILY EVENTS.

180-181 An elaborate hairstyle of tiny braids curled in silver and a bright purple veil complete the clothing of this young Tuareg woman from In Gall and her companions as they enliven a tribal gathering with the sound of tambourines. Women play an important role in Tuareg society, which was originally matriarchal. Repositories of tradition, their opinion is always respected.

182 The *TARIK,* or Tuareg camel saddle, is made of wood and has a back rest with a cross in front, sometimes brass-plated. The various types of saddles can be distinguished by their quality, the color of the leather decorations, the metal trinkets adorning them, and their sturdiness.

182–183 A single donkey can transport all the possessions of these women from the Air region of Niger. Their baggage includes cotton cloth, mats, and colored leather bags.

184 AND 185 Makeup requires mutual cooperation, as shown in this photo taken in the Air region of Niger (left). Colors are obtained using mixtures of mineral pigments such as antimony, which is used to line the eyes (right).

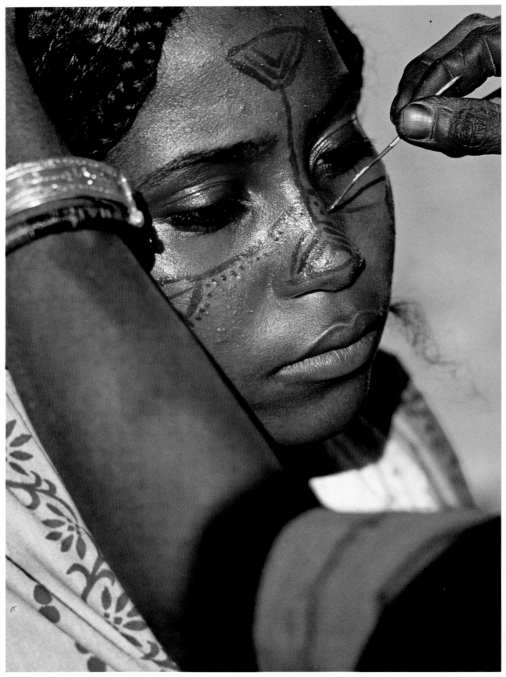

186–187 These Tuareg from Ghadames, Libya, are elegantly dressed for a traditional festival, but have replaced the indigo-dyed *tagilmust* with a checked Arabian shawl, which is sturdier and much less costly.

187 TOP A group of Tuareg perform a traditional dance at the Ghadames Festival. Many Libyan Tuareg have now become sedentary members of modern society and work in the tourist industry.

187 BOTTOM AND 188–189 The rhythmic thud of the drum, accompanied by songs and endless litanies during the Ghadames Festival, is part of every Tuareg festival or family ceremony. The instrument is often just a skin stretched over a wooden mortar.

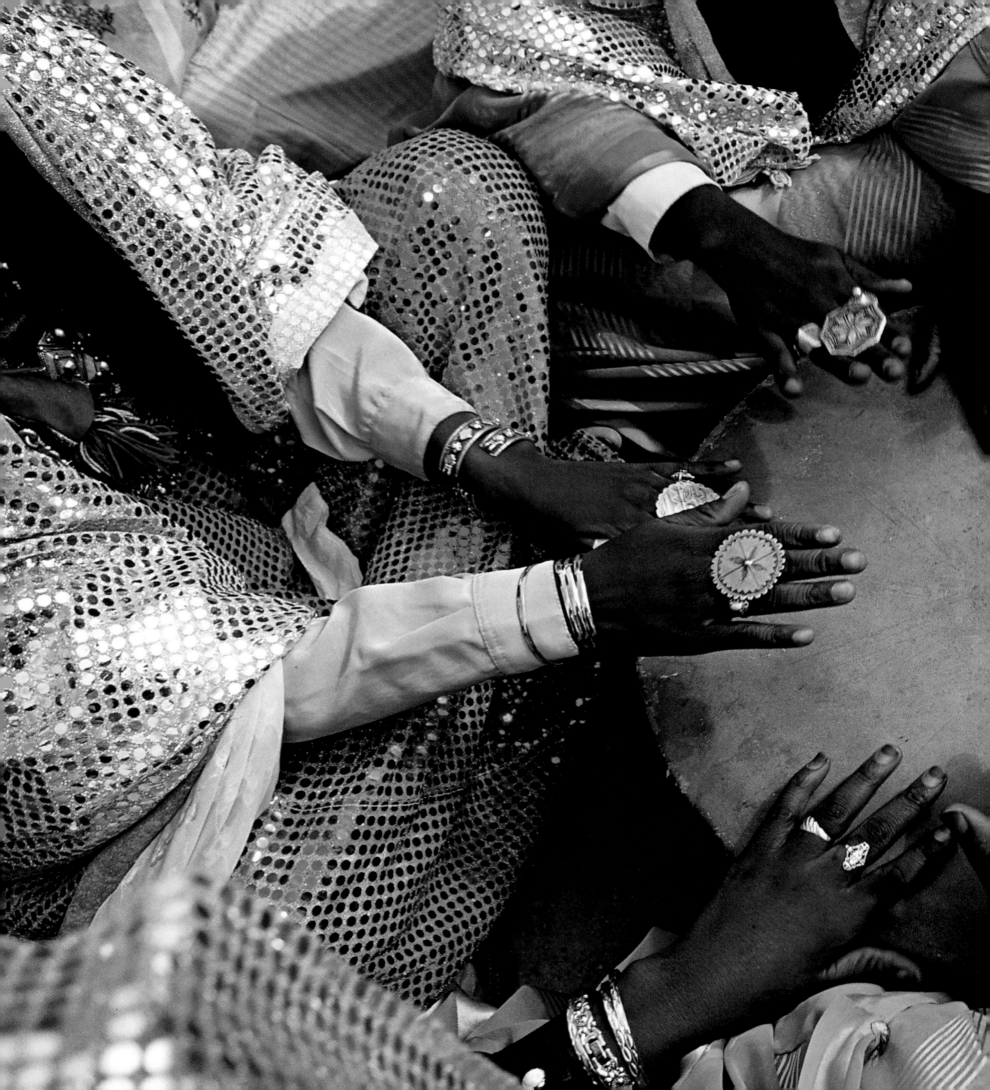

190 TOP AND BOTTOM

Stoic and indifferent to their own suffering and that of others, Tebu camel drivers can make extremely long, perilous voyages across the desert, ignoring thirst and fatigue.

191 As resources in the Tibesti and surrounding regions grow more scarce, the Tebu are forced into incessant nomadism. Women are not immune from daily fatigues, and they rarely have a chance to steal a bit of rest in the shade of the hut. Gathering and trading salt, which is deposited on the bottom of old craters, is one of the primary activities of Tebu living in the Trou au Natron region.

192 AND 193 The ancestors of these Bideyat girls from the Ennedi region in Chad may have founded the Kanem-Bornu kingdom, which at its height in the fifteenth century extended from Tripolitania to north of Cameroon. In reality, the Bideyat are a mosaic of peoples united by a close linguistic heritage.

THE NOMADS OF CHAD

The influence of the Tuareg extends east to the 14th meridian. This is more than just a virtual boundary: the territory of the Tebu, the so-called black nomads of the Sahara, begins past the oases of Kawar and Tenéré. The Tebu have very black skin but do not have Negroid features. They are thought to be the descendants of indigenous Neolithic peoples who interbred with whites from the Nile Valley. Their harsh, guttural language is unrelated to Berber, and its origins are unknown. The Tebu, about 200,000 persons, live in the Tibesti. This constantly moving population is widely dispersed due to the precarious living conditions offered by the environment and their ferocious individualism, a feature peculiar to Tebu society. In the Tibesti, the scarcity of resources does not permit stable settlements: in the entire massif, there are only a dozen small oases and only 50,000 date-producing palms (some oases in the Algerian Sahara have 200,000 trees). The Tebu boast that they can walk for days on end without food and very little water, exceeding the stoicism of any other inhabitants of the Sahara. They consider cattle stealing to be a right, and murder (outside their own clan) an act of bravado. Feuds and vendettas can go on for years, or at least until one of the parties gives up by paying heavy reparations in livestock. Tebu women are certainly no angels either: they carry daggers hidden beneath their clothing and do not hesitate to shame their husbands by stripping in front of guests. This total materialism leaves no room for religion or poetry, which are considered useless. Tebu society, continually spun around by ceaseless nomadism, dispersed throughout a vast territory, answers only to the authority of clans, which in turn are subject to a supreme authority, the *dardai*. The approximately forty clans are patrilineal: members of the same group have a common pasture territory, answer to common laws, and brand camels with a special mark. The civil war that has devastated the Tibesti for twenty years does not seem to have changed the traditional equilibrium of Tebu society, and in fact, the conflict seems to have paradoxically strengthened it: with the interruption of supplies by truck from the south, caravans have picked up the slack. The presence of occupying troops in the area has caused traffic to increase, and raiding has once again become a lawful activity, or at least can no longer be prosecuted.

The opportunistic and pragmatic Tebu have been able to exploit the situation to their advantage. The Bideyat of the Ennedi region, around ten thousand people divided into clans, have equally mysterious origins. They emigrated a few hundred years ago from the Sudanese Darfur and from several regions in northern Chad, and are seminomadic farmers who mainly concentrate on growing various seasonal food crops, particularly millet.

THE MAURI

While the Tebu and the Tuareg, secure in their mountains, have maintained their ethnic identity, the western Berber tribes, known as the Mauri, have instead borne the full brunt of Islamization, which they have accepted with a sort of mystic ardor. The Mauri are a mixture of Arab and Berber blood, with contributions from the dark-skinned peoples who populated the Sahara in the Neolithic period. They speak Arabic, although some isolated tribes are still bilingual, and many names of places, plants, and animals are Berber in origin. Mauri tribes, united by religious and warrior traditions, are divided into an extremely complicated hierarchy, with a framework of social divisions that is theoretically permanent: nobles, vassals, servants, artisans, musicians, and storytellers. In reality, movements between one class and another are not only possible but frequent. As with the Tuareg, sedentary farmers of the oases are black Africans and hold the lowest place in society. Nobles and vassal tribes raise livestock, which in the Sahara automatically means a nomadic life. The extent of migrations in search of pastures and water varies based on the territory and the frequency of rain. In years of bad drought, these movements can cover thousands of miles, as in the case of the Reguibat, who wander an area between the former Spanish

Sahara and southern Mauritania. Ascetic and frugal, these nomads draw their sustenance primarily from millet, dates, and milk. Animals are rarely slaughtered and meat is consumed only on special occasions. Despite Arab influence, Mauri women retain a surprising degree of autonomy and can take great liberties without incurring social sanctions. Divorces and repudiations are common, with the primary cause being female jealousy of the husband's occasional mistresses. The dictates of Islam are fully followed with regard to work, however: matrons of the noble classes do absolutely nothing except ensure their obesity by guzzling down milk (there are special high-calorie diets whose secrets are passed down from mother to daughter). In the nomad world, which is always on the edge of malnutrition, it is understandable that obesity is synonymous with female beauty. The Mauri also include two residual groups that occupy highly specialized production niches: the Nemadi and the Imraguen. The Nemadi, no more than five hundred people, are antelope hunters who live in the desert region between the dunes of Djouf and the wells of Araouane, west of the city of Oualata. The Imraguen, who are dark-skinned seminomadic fishermen, are located near Cape Timiris on the Atlantic coast.

198 TOP The women in this Peul village are busy smoking fish (left) and threshing millet in wooden mortars (center). The Peul, or Fulani, occupy a vast swathe of West Africa south of the Sahara from Senegal to Chad. Totally converted to Islam, in general they have abandoned nomadic herding and have either moved to cities or devoted themselves to agriculture in villages that are traditionally built around a mosque (right).

198 BOTTOM AND 199 Peul clothing varies depending on the region and economic conditions. Wealthy women wear heavy gold earrings (bottom), while men like this young inhabitant of a village along the Niger River enhance their elegance with brightly colored *cheche* scarves.

THE PEUL

The eastern part of the desert is practically uninhabited, at least until the Nile Valley. Here, in the region between the river and the Red Sea, live the Beja—goat, cattle, and dromedary herders. The family is the center of their society, which is fragmented into small, constantly moving groups. The Beja have always strongly defended their independence, which is based on errant herding, something they were practicing as early as three thousand years ago, when they were first cited in Egyptian chronicles. The Chaamba of northern Algeria, who live near the oases of Ouargla and El Golea, are also nomads of pure Arabic origin. Once known for their ferocious predations, they now have become skilled livestock breeders and traders. They live in camel wool tents similar to those of the Bedouin of Saudi Arabia. The Mozabites, a quintessential Berber and Sahara people, have a long history of religious persecution and diaspora. Their five cities—Ghardaia, El Atteuf, Beni Isguen, Bou Noura, and Melika—stand on the steep banks of Wadi Mzab in Algeria. The Mozabites, considered the purest of Muslims, have very rigid customs: music and luxuries are prohibited, and the faithful may not drink or smoke. The condition of women is quite different from that of the Tuareg or Mauri, even though those groups are greatly influenced by Islam: in the Mzab, women have few rights and many duties. Commerce and business are a true lifestyle choice for the Mozabites that actually requires some sort of initiation. At a certain age, young people must leave Mzab and may only return home when they have accumulated a sufficient amount of money.

A picture of Sahara populations would not be complete without mentioning the Peul, who in reality live in the Sahel region from Senegal to Chad but have strong, ancient bonds to the desert. There are excellent reasons for believing that the origins of the Peul should be sought in the Sahara, among those Neolithic herders depicted in the rock paintings of the Bovidian era. Some of the scenes painted on the sandstone of Tassili n'Ajjer in fact bear a surprising resemblance to their traditions and mythology. In Peul villages, domestic space is organized according to clear rules based on the cardinal points and family hierarchy. Women's homes are in the section facing east, and are separated from the livestock area by a so-called calf cord, where young animals are tied to separate them from the rest of the herd. This scheme is also clearly and meticulously detailed in the frescoes of Tissoukai. The same site also shows a cross-section of a hut, in which we see a surface on which a series of pots and recipients are carefully arranged. This is a Bororo women's *kaakul*, a display of cooking utensils received as wedding gifts that are exhibited for the admiration of relatives when a new village is founded. In Uan Derbaouen and Tin Tazarift, again in the Tassili, there are representations of oxen being carefully groomed as they stand in the water; until recent times this was the custom of the *lotori* rite, a ceremony that celebrated the origins of the domestication of cattle. Most of the Peul, who are devout Muslims, now lead sedentary lives related to trade or a mixed economy based on animals and agriculture.

THE BORORO

200 TOP AND BOTTOM   The Bororo are proud of their beasts, which can endure long transhumances under incredibly difficult conditions. The zebu is a sturdy animal but it produces very little milk—yet its beauty makes the Bororo prefer it over other more productive animals.

201 LEFT AND RIGHT   In Bororo society, the wife is the head of the household, and no husband would ever dare give her orders in public. Marriage is considered temporary and divorce is available to both spouses. The strongest family bonds are between mother and children.

The Bororo (around sixty thousand people) have maintained their nomadic lifestyle, wandering with their herds through the steppelike plains of southern Niger, near the border with Nigeria; it's an arid, inhospitable environment, where resources are scarce. The movements of the Bororo, on their constant search for water and new pastures, never cease. Their eternal roaming leaves hardly any traces on the ground: the only remaining evidence of their settlements are the frames of the semicircular tents, which are little more than basic shelters made from branches, and a few enclosures made with thorny branches for the livestock, which is the nomadic farmer's sole wealth and reason for existence. During the long months of the dry season, the groups disperse across the territory, and conviviality is reduced to a minimum: the essential thing is to survive until the first rains. When the rains arrive, the ponds fill up again, and the grass grows again out of the dust like a miracle, life changes completely: this is the time of the great ceremonial gatherings and dances, *yake* and *geerewol*, where young people have the opportunity to get to know and court each other. Beauty is a fundamental element of Bororo culture and is based on set attributes: height; a long, straight nose; light skin; and bright teeth and eyes. Life is hard for unattractive people, even though they can take advantage of other gifts, such as singing or dancing ability or intelligence, which are almost as important as physical appearance. The movements and clothing of men are carefully designed to be pleasing: sometimes they contort their faces into grotesque grimaces, their eyes bulging and mouths open, to show off their white teeth. It is a beauty contest in the truest sense of the word, a parade for the female members of the audience, who watch the show with the utmost attention. Then, at the end of the festival, the young women pick their gallant men and the pairs leave the crowd for the bushes, where they consummate their engagement. In the meantime, the elders reforge alliances among the clans and organize future migrations, following the ritual that governs the eternal repetition of pastoral existence.

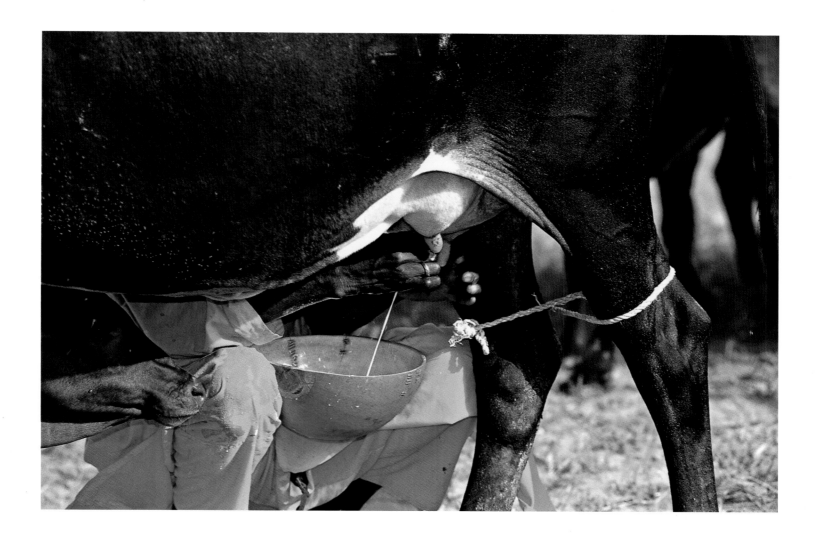

202 AND 203 Activities revolving around the care of livestock occupy most of the day in Bororo society, and all members of the family are involved. By the time they are six years old, children know how to look after a herd. The Bororo are almost completely dependent on cows, which produce an average of two to three quarts of milk a day. Fresh milk is collected in containers made of large, hollowed-out squashes. Fresh, curdled, or dried, it is an integral part of the herders' diet.

204 AND 205 During the wet season, the Bororo constantly move in search of pastures. After unloading the furniture, the herders prepare to set up their new camp and the livestock enclosures.

206 AND 207 Even in day-to-day life, young Bororo women (left) and men do not neglect their appearance. This young man's straw and leather hat, with its traditional conical shape (right), is adorned with ostrich feathers.

208 AND 209 Young Bororo prepare for the Geerewol.

210–211 The young men of the group line up to perform a series of dances in which they compete for beauty.

212 AND 213 To accentuate their beauty, the Bororo roll their eyes, show their teeth and gums, and make their cheeks and lips vibrate (left).

214–215 The Geerewol is performed primarily in the late afternoon and evening, and often Tuareg from nearby camps are invited to watch.

LIVING IN THE SAHARA

216 (CLOCKWISE FROM TOP LEFT) PALMS ON THE EDGE OF AN ERG MARK THE BORDER BETWEEN INHABITED AREAS AND THE DESERT. A SALT CARAVAN SWAYS THROUGH THE SANDS OF MAURITANIA. THE "BLACK TENT" IS TYPICAL OF NOMADS OF THE NORTHERN SAHARA. SOLID, STUDDED DOORS PROTECT THE PRIVACY OF THE INHABITANTS OF TIMBUKTU, MALI.

217 INTER-SAHARA TRADE, ESPECIALLY ON A SMALL SCALE, IS STILL PRIMARILY HANDLED BY CARAVANS, WHICH ENSURE EXTREMELY LOW TRANSPORT COSTS.

218 AND 219 THE PRESENCE OF WATER AND FEATURES OF THE TERRITORY HAVE GREATLY INFLUENCED HUMAN SETTLEMENTS IN THE SAHARA. TROGLODYTE DWELLINGS AND THE PALM GROVES OF MATMATA, TUNISIA (BOTTOM LEFT AND CENTER), SHARPLY CONTRAST WITH THE TWIG HUTS SCATTERED IN THE TEGUEDEI OASIS IN CHAD (BOTTOM RIGHT), WHOSE MONOCHROME LANDSCAPE IS ENLIVENED BY THE UNUSUAL PRESENCE OF A LAKE SURROUNDED BY SPOTS OF VEGETATION (RIGHT).

220–221 SURROUNDED BY A SEA OF DUNES, THIS LITTLE LAKE IS ONE OF THE MANY PONDS THAT DOT THE LIBYAN SAHARA NEAR THE SEBHA OASIS IN FEZZAN.

222–223 SOME OF THE PERMANENT BASINS OF WATER IN THE SO-CALLED LAKE AREA OF LIBYA ARE BORDERED BY LUXURIANT VEGETATION.

A LAND OF WANDERERS

Until colonial times, a dense network of trading routes traversed the Sahara from the Mediterranean to black Africa. Like a dry ocean, the great desert was plied by fleets of caravans, loaded with gold, ivory, salt, foodstuffs, and luxury goods. The transport specialists were nomads, warriors, and camel herders. Great market cities, rich and powerful, sprang up on the two shores of the Sahara. Oases became the ports of call, places for refueling and production, like islands in the sea. The remains of this past include cities and fortresses, some in ruins, others still vital, like Timbuktu and Agadez. Complex hydraulic structures have survived, along with palm groves and vegetable gardens coaxed from the sand through tenacious daily labor. Salt caravans wind slowly along the ancient routes. This terri-

search for resources: this is a land of nomads (from the Greek *nomàs*, "wanderers"). Nomadism, based on a close relationship between man and his animals, is the only way to exploit this fragile, arid ecosystem. Livestock transforms grass into valuable protein, providing shepherds with many of the products they need to survive, with an extremely high ecological yield. The key animal for all nomadic civilizations in the Sahara is the dromedary, which is not only a living storehouse of resources, but a primary, irreplaceable means of transportation. Its resistance to thirst and fatigue has given it a crucial role in the trans-Saharan caravan trade. Nomads and sedentary peoples have necessarily developed diametrically opposed mentalities and cultures, and over the course of history they

often have competed with each other. In the Sahara, however, more than elsewhere, the two worlds have never been completely closed to each other. Rather, there has been a relationship of collaboration and mutual convenience. The constellation of fortified villages that bounds the northern lip of the desert has never been so much a line of defense

tory is still a land of caravans and animal herds, its borders invisible and its center the tent, an emblem of nomadic life. Except in peripheral regions near the large flood plains of the Niger, Senegal, and Nile Rivers, agriculture is impracticable in the Sahara. The only place in the desert where sedentary life is possible is the oases, where an incredibly hostile environment has been domesticated with astonishing skill. These oases, sporadic by nature, are marked by an abrupt contrast with the surrounding landscape. Boundaries are sharp and brutal: brilliant green palm groves are immediately followed by an empty mineral waste. With the exception of these islands, living in the Sahara means moving ceaselessly in an incessant

as a zone for trade and communication. The great cosmopolitan cities of the south at the edges of the savanna served the same purpose. So the Sahara has always been an open complex whose function was (and to a certain extent still is) based on the integration of oases, trading cities, and caravan transport, all crucial, interdependent nodes within the system. For centuries, this mechanism guaranteed the prosperity of desert peoples; it created the human geography of the Sahara, determined the form and nature of its settlements, and traced the maps for the production and handling of commercial products. And above all, it ensured a lifestyle whose demise, after two thousand years of history, now seems inevitable.

224 PROTECTED BY THE SHADY CROWN OF A PALM, AN ALGERIAN TUAT FARMER CAREFULLY LOOKS AFTER HIS FIELDS, WHICH CAN ASSURE HIM MORE THAN ONE HARVEST A YEAR.

225 TOP LEFT AND CENTER THESE TWO IMAGES OF THE LIBYAN SAHARA SUMMARIZE THE CONTRADICTORY NATURE OF THE DESERT, AN IMMENSE EXPANSE OF STERILE EARTH PUNCTUATED BY OASES. THE GREEK GEOGRAPHER STRABO COMPARED IT TO A PANTHER SKIN.

FARMERS

OF THE SAND

Agriculture has two fundamental needs: fertile soil and, most important, water. In the Sahara it almost never rains and surface water is practically nonexistent. Thus, cultivation of food plants depends entirely on the rational exploitation of underground water resources. The oasis, an artificial microcosm, is the culmination of this process of taming the environment. In the immensity of the desert, oases account for almost nothing: all the palm groves of Algeria, which alone contain half the date palms in the Sahara, are located in an area the size of a few counties. The oasis is not a natural phenomenon, but the product of tenacious, endless work. The oases of the Sahara were born to meet the needs of trans-Sahara trade, which required stable, reliable supply centers: areas of trade and communication, like land-locked harbors in the great dry sea of the desert. The first settlements, which developed around already existing wells, took the form of fortified stone enclosures, built on high ground

whenever possible. This type of citadel, or *ksar*, can be found in almost every oasis in the Sahara. The maze of lanes, tunnels, stairways, terraces, and inner courtyards reveals a dual purpose: defense and protection of society, while remaining open to the nomadic, ever-moving outside world. Within the ksar, an invisible web of connections between house and house, courtyard and courtyard, is superimposed on the map of public ways. Family life unfolds along these passages, which are often underground and far from the indiscreet eye. The outer walls of the citadel create a border, but it is not impenetrable: the doors facing outward lead to reception areas for strangers, and transit and entertainment zones. But it is the palm grove, at the edge of human habitation, that represents the true point of contact with the outside world: here is where business contacts are made with nomads, who camp in the desert at a distance established by unwritten law. We can distinguish different types of oases: their con-

225 TOP RIGHT BUILT AT THE EDGE OF A HARSH PLATEAU, THE DEAD CITY OF DJADO IN NORTHEASTERN NIGER IS SURROUNDED BY THE WALLS OF AN ANCIENT, RUINED FORTRESS.

225 BOTTOM THE BRILLIANT GREEN PALM GROVES AND CULTIVATED FIELDS OF TAMERZA, TUNISIA, STAND OUT LIKE A LITTLE EDEN BETWEEN THE BARE MOUNTAINS THAT SURROUND THE OASIS.

226 Captured by underground channels or drawn from open water holes like this one in Air, Niger, water must be distributed equally (left). For this purpose, in the Timimoun oasis in Algeria (right), the cracks in the *kesria* establish the share of water for each farmer.

227 **TOP** The valleys that furrow the arid southern slopes of the Moroccan Atlas Mountains are distinctively Saharan in appearance. In the oases, irrigated by the waters of wadis, a thick canopy of palm trees overlooks olive, fig, almond, and fruit trees and vegetables of every kind.

227 **BOTTOM** The Berber villages that punctuate the Oued Draa valley in Morocco hold the remains of ancient mud brick fortifications built as a defense against desert nomads.

formation and the position of villages and crops are closely linked to landscape features and water use. Wadi oases are generally located parallel to the riverbed, which holds the gardens and date palm plantations. The largest group of this type of oasis extends in a straight line along the Saoura valley, which runs along the buttresses of Hammada del Guir and the Great Western Erg, continuing into the Tuat region. The enormous expanse of dunes, which runs to the slopes of the Sahara Atlas, supplies excellent drinking water, which is drained and transported to the village through a network of underground channels called *foggaras,* a

masterpiece of hydraulic technology. The foggaras capture the underground waters of the erg and, using the force of gravity, carry it to the place desired. The conduits, which have an elliptical shape and are large enough to allow a person to pass through them, are maintained through constant effort. The pure water supplied by foggaras is used solely for household needs. Crops are irrigated with moderately saline water from the subsoil of the river, extracted using typical hand-operated jack wells known as *khottaras.* The foggara system is especially refined in oases on the shores of dried lakes, where the incline is imperceptible. The cen-

228 The El-Faiyum oasis is in a depression south of the Giza area and was once occupied by a great lake, now considerably shrunken (left). Ancient and modern agricultural techniques coexist in this area, one of the most productive and densely populated in Egypt (right).

229 Usually the surface waters of the Sahara are too mineralized for irrigation, as we can see in the lakes of Fezzan (left) and the Siwa oasis (center), while in places like Tichitt, Mauritania (right), rain is collected in short-lived lakes to permit seasonal agriculture.

230–231 Except for the minaret, the tallest structure in the village, the buildings of Tichitt almost completely blend in with the arid escarpment of Dhar Oualata.

232–233 and 234–235 As shown in these details photographed in Oualata (232 bottom) and Chinguetti, Mauritania (232 top and 233), and the passageways in the Berber village of Chenini, Tunisia (234–235)—which are so narrow that only one person at a time can walk through them—the intricate architecture of Sahara villages meets a triple need: to protect privacy, shelter the inhabitants from the harsh weather, and prevent attacks by marauders.

tral portion of the *sebkha,* with its layer of salt outcroppings, is in fact unusable for crops, which are limited to a slender edge around the basin. In Timimoun, in the Gourara region, the tunnels extend out into the subsoil for miles, parallel to the banks of the sebkha, capturing along the way the underground streams that supply the bottom of the depression. At the mouth of the oasis, the water is collected in a large basin, where the first allocation of shares for each family is made. A special device, called the *kesria,* consisting of a specially drilled stone slab, closes off the side of the basin facing the crops. Calculating the volume of water

enclosed garden. The same concept is expressed in the Christian garden of Eden and the Arabic *jennat,* a term which in the Sahara means cultivated fields. But the oases of the ergs are where the concept of paradise, as opposed to the destructive, hellish desert, becomes most powerful and clear. Situated entirely among the dunes, these oases do not owe their survival to foggaras or other systems of manual irrigation. The Souf region, among the sands of the Great Eastern Erg, appears to be dotted with craters with dark green crowns of the palm trees rising from them. In the Souf, water lies just under the surface, submerged by tons of sand.

To plant, you need to dig holes large and deep enough to allow the roots of the palms to reach the water table. The edges of these circular depressions are surrounded by fences of palm fronds; this creates artificial dunes that protect the oasis from the leveling action of the wind. The ecology of erg oases is based entirely on date palms, the true queen of

assigned to the various owners, which depends on the size of the notches in the kesria, is extremely complex. When the allocation has been made, a network of open ditches directs the water to the gardens. The dense network of palm fronds holds and retains nighttime humidity, creating a niche of temperate climate. All kinds of vegetables and Mediterranean fruit trees grow in this natural greenhouse, including figs, peaches, apricots, oranges, and pomegranates. The abundance of water often allows harvesting more than once a year. This is the ancient Persian *pairidaeza,* or

the Sahara. "With its feet in water and its head in the fire of the sky," according to an Arab proverb, *Phoenix dactylifera* is a miraculous plant. The origins of its cultivation are unknown, but certainly date back to very ancient times. A Babylonian treatise explained its usefulness, extolling 360 different ways of using it. For thousands of years, its fruit has been a staple for entire populations. Sahara peoples have at least twenty-five ways of distinguishing different types of dates, depending on form, size, pulp consistency, and color. Dates are a high-energy food, and most

important, they are always available. Properly dried and pressed into bars, dates keep for a long time, becoming an indispensable food supply for long trips into the desert. The precious trunk is often the only source of wood available: cut into boards, it is used to build roofs, doors, and windows. The strong, flexible branches are excellent supports for roofs and arches, or are used to form the framework for ceilings, which are then covered with plaster or unbaked earth. The fibrous leaves are used to weave mats and baskets. The fermented lymph produces an invigorating drink known as palm wine. The subsistence of the large rural population of the Souf, a third of that in the Algerian Sahara, is closely linked to palm cultivation. The urban oases of Mzab, in northern Algeria, are indubitably the finest result of human adaptation in the Sahara. The plateau that delimits El Oued Mzab is one of the worst places imaginable to live: the rocky terrain, riddled with ravines and gorges, makes communication difficult; the water table is very deep, up to four hundred feet; during the summer, temperatures can easily reach 120°F; rainfall is scarce, perhaps fifteen days a year at the most. Yet its inhabitants have succeeded in transforming this desolation into a practically perfect place to live. The 200,000 palms and the gardens, which occupy the banks of the dry river, require large quantities of water. The hydraulic system on which the prosperity of Mzab is based is made of a series of underground dams, which block the course of the wadi and its tributaries, feeding the great underground reservoirs that form the geological structure of the plateau. Over three thousand wells reach the water table: some are extremely deep, up to three hundred feet, and digging them may have required decades of work. Irrigation of the oasis is performed by a network of channels that runs directly from the collection basins, crosses the kesria, and reaches the croplands. There is a deep, complete rec-

onciliation between the natural environment and the dwellings. In Mzab, spiritual and practical needs merge harmoniously, expressing themselves in the outlines of the urban plan and the design of private homes, based on austerity and intimacy. The market economy has made crucial changes in the Mozabite social and production system, although the constant cash flow from business activities has allowed the population to retain at least a semblance of its distinctive traditions. Other oases have been less fortunate: punished by their geographic position, overpopulated or cut out of the new national communications network, they are suffering a picturesque decline. Djanet, Ghadames, and the oases of Teneré and Mauritania, once important caravan stops, have now been relegated to the margins of Sahara society, visited only by the occasional careless, hurried tourist. Yet others, like Touggourt and Ouargla, have endured brutal conversions that have erased the original outlines of the settlement. Ouargla has become a service center for the oil city of Hassi Messaoud, with unchecked, destructive urbanization. New towns, completely removed from the environment and surrounded by rusted wreckage, stand in places where the nomadic tribes of the area once camped. Arlit, in Niger, is a classic example of a twentieth-century oasis, an artificial transplant of a "European" city right in the middle of the desert, created to meet needs that are completely foreign to the local communities. Built from scratch in 1971 to exploit enormous uranium deposits, it stands on a desolate plain. Bars, swimming pools, restaurants, and hotels are strictly reserved for mining personnel, who live separately like an alien colony, with no relationship to the world around them. The concept of an oasis as a trading area where the economic and human resources of the Sahara can be metabolized has been completely turned on its head.

236 The Ghadames oasis in northwestern Libya is located in a strategic position along the caravan route that ran from Tripoli to Lake Chad. In the past, it played a leading role in trans-Sahara trade. Its inhabitants have retained many original features of ancient Berber culture.

237 LEFT The complex topography of Ghadames unravels in an apparently irregular manner, following tortuous paths adorned with arches.

237 RIGHT According to local belief, the crenellation that dominates the terraces of Ghadames protects against evil influences.

238–239 Once an important caravan junction, the Siwa oasis surrounds the fortified village, a thick cluster of mud brick structures, now falling into ruins.

240 This Tuareg caravan driver, walking with his dromedaries through the immense Niger Teneré, does hard, risky work in one of the most difficult environments in the world.

241 TOP In the Sahara, the caravan economy survives where there is no interest in creating a modern communications network. The subsistence of communities in these areas depends almost totally on the slow, measured gait of the dromedary.

CARAVANS

AND THE SALT ROADS

With the arrival of the Arabs, the Sahara became part of that international system of far-flung trade that linked the Islamic world from Morocco to Indonesia. The two sides of the Sahara were connected by a network of roads running north to south, crossing a series of intermediate stops: production sites for food-stuffs and salt mining centers. Salt, common in the Sahara but rare and precious in black Africa, was traded for gold and agricultural products of the savanna. In addition to gold and salt, the range of goods traded was quite vast: from the Sahara terminals came dates, Venetian glass pearls, iron and tin wire, sheets of bronze, calico and silk from India, paper, and finished marble from Andalusia. Tropical Africa supplied slaves, ivory, ostrich feathers, perfumed resins, and other exotic and luxury articles. The most important routes ran between Morocco, Tunis, and Tripoli. Not only caravans made the great crossing. In the oases, which acted as a springboard for the great leap southward, the caravans were unpacked and put together again, divided into various sections with dif-

ferent destinations. Due to its geographical position, the Tuat region was the best known of these junctions, an extremely important place for gathering and sorting goods from Mediterranean ports and the Beléd-es-Sudàn. The Libyan oases of Murzuch, Ghat, and Gadhames and the towns of Tichitt and Ouadane in Mauritania played the same role. The same scheme was followed on the southern shore of the Sahara: on the Niger River, however, it was the pirogue that acted as intermediary between the terminals of Timbuktu and Gao and the mercantile cities of the inland delta.

One of the most heavily traveled routes ran from Fez to Marrakech, reaching Sigilmassa. From here, the caravans once again departed for the salt mines of Teghaza and Taoudeni, where goods were again sorted, and then to Oualata and Timbuktu. The roads that crossed western Mauritania and those leading to the oases of Libya also ended in Timbuktu, crossing the Hoggar and Djanet. Tunis was regularly connected to the

241 BOTTOM Although modest, this caravan moving across the dunes of Chiriet, in Niger, is a perfect mobile unit capable of going for long periods without provisions.

242 The transport of salt in Mali, shown in both photos here, is handled primarily by the Berabich, a professional caste comprised of various ethnic groups, predominantly Mauri. In Taoudeni, 500 miles north of Timbuktu, the mineral is extracted and cut into slabs, each one weighing about sixty-five pounds.

243 TOP AND BOTTOM The little oasis of Fachi acts as an intermediary stop along the salt road, which runs through Teneré from Bilma to Agadez. Even today, thousands of dromedaries loaded with salt complete this 375-mile route in a couple of weeks. Salt is packaged in wooden molds with a strange truncated cone form that is completely unsuitable for packaging and transport, although the Tuareg seem to pay no heed to this problem.

Tuat and especially Gadhames, an important stop from which the caravan route to Ghat and Djanet departed, continuing to Agadez, the terminal for trade with the Haoussa states of Kano and Katsina. In turn, Agadez was connected to Gao and the salt mines of Kawar, where the road that linked Fezzan to Lake Chad ran. To the east, trade was primarily along the Nile. Transverse routes across the Darfur and Libyan desert were too long and difficult, and were soon abandoned for the easier coastal route, which from Tripoli ran to the Siwa oasis and then Cairo. The caravans that still follow the ancient routes across the Sahara are now limited to transporting salt

Sahara trade is no longer trans-Sahara, but it continues to exist, because in many areas of the desert, it is simply more convenient. The old Taoudeni salt route, like many others, continues to be traveled by hundreds of small caravans that supply a flourishing market along the entire middle course of the Niger. Salt is no longer worth its weight in gold, but has remained a strategic staple. Unlike sea salt, which is considered to be of poor quality, the rock salt mined in the Sahara is said to have miraculous properties for both animals and man. The most prized salt is from Amadror, while that of Taoudeni is known for its curative qualities. In sheets, blocks, or pressed bars, sawed into pieces or ground into coarse granules, this precious mineral reaches markets all over tropical Africa. A throng of brokers, small merchants, pirogue boatmen and dealers, and their families, live on these transactions. In the Sahara, the salt mines are more or less all located around the Tropic of Cancer in remote, inaccessible areas: Idjil and Tichitt in Mauritania; Teghaza and Taoudeni in Mali; Bilma, Fachi, Séguedine, and Teguid-

and other staples, primarily dates and millet. But contrary to appearances, the caravan economy is anything but dead. In the Sahara and the Sahel, the celebrated cash economy affects only a handful of persons: everyone else—millions of people—lives on the products of their fields or animals. They are the caravan customers. Truck transport requires a road network that can be used in any season and is based on market laws: it must be quick and remunerative enough to amortize the high cost of fuel and vehicle maintenance, a condition that is not always met in Africa. The caravan works on other principles. Duration of transport is unimportant, nor does it increase handling costs. The death of a dromedary does not threaten the success of the operation, and the dead animal is not a total loss: it is recycled, transforming into meat and products useful to the nomad economy. All in all, camels cost less than trucks.

dam Tessoum in Niger; and Bedo and Démi in Chad are only a few of the most important. Transport of the mineral is entrusted almost entirely to the caravans, self-sufficient, mobile structures that can go for long periods without provisions. A camel not only carries goods on its back, but everything else needed: water, food, and shelter. Caravan efficiency is not limited by animals, but by man. A dromedary can carry up to about 330 pounds and can walk indefinitely. The enormous *mehari* of the Tuareg, once used for distant forays, can travel 125 miles a day on any kind of terrain. On the sand, they are at least as efficient as a motorized vehicle, if not more. And they consume no fuel. As a man can lead many camels, the advantages are clear. Caravans function according to an extremely efficient mechanism that is worth exploring in detail. Each year, when the winter season arrives, the Tuareg of Air leave for the salt mines of Bilma, 300 miles to the west, past Tenerè.

244 AND 245 A reddish, granular salt is extracted by evaporation from the Fachi salt mine wells, which are full of a supersaturated solution. Extraction is done by the Kanuri, a dark-skinned people who were once slaves of the Tuareg.

246–247 EXTRACTED FROM THE SEBKHA NORTH OF MAURITANIA, THE SALT TRANSPORTED BY THIS CARAVAN ACROSS THE COUNTRY'S ENDLESS STRETCHES OF SAND IS HEADED TO THE MARKETS OF SENEGAL AND MALI.

247 TOP THESE DROMEDARIES MUST CARRY THEIR BURDENS, WEIGHING ALMOST 335 POUNDS, TO TIMBUKTU, A TWENTY-DAY MARCH FROM TAOUDENI.

247 BOTTOM TRANSPORT ALONG THE TAOUDENI SALT ROAD REQUIRES THE LOAD TO BE CHECKED FREQUENTLY: IF THE SLABS OF SALT ARRIVE DAMAGED, THEY LOSE THEIR VALUE.

248, 249, AND 250–251 THE IMMENSE SAHARA STILL MAKES WAY FOR CARAVAN TRANSPORT: EVERY YEAR THOUSANDS OF DROMEDARIES TRAVEL BETWEEN FACHI AND BILMA.

252–253 DUSK CAPTURES A SOLITARY CAMEL DRIVER ON THE SOBOROM VALLEY ROAD IN THE TIBESTI: IN THE SAHARA, MAN AND DROMEDARY ARE AN INSEPARABLE UNIT.

254–255 A LARGE CARAVAN HEADS TOWARD THE SALT MINES OF BILMA, NIGER, LOADED WITH TRADING GOODS AND AGRICULTURAL PRODUCE, WHICH WILL BE BARTERED FOR CAKES OF SALT.

SHIPS OF THE DESERT

A typical caravan comprises ten men and a hundred camels. The load essentially consists of millet and cotton cloth, which is bartered for bars of salt. The salt is extracted by evaporation, when still moist, it is pulverized in mortars and then pressed into wooden molds with a strange, truncated cone shape. The cakes, which weigh about thirty pounds each, are packaged in palm leaf mats and elaborately tied to the pack saddles. In addition to salt, the caravans carry supplies of water, dates, and dromedary dung, which will be used as cooking fuel during the trip. Each camel carries from four to six cakes of salt, the necessary victuals, a couple of leather skins or bladder bags full of water, a bit of forage, and the baggage, for a total of about 250 to 300 pounds.

The first few hours of travel are extremely important, a true technical shakedown period that will determine the success of the operation. The caravan leader orders the knots on the pack saddles to be adjusted, and everyone ensures that things are running smoothly. The rhythm of the gait is controlled to maintain an average of two to three miles per hour. Each man leads a line of ten dromedaries, tied to each other by uniform lengths of rope. The camels are rarely ridden: most of the day the Tuareg go on foot, step after step through the yielding, scorching sand. By the time they make camp, darkness has already long fallen. On the way out, the signal to stop comes with the setting of the constellation Orion, which the Tuareg call *amanar*, or "the guide." On the return trip, Venus, the first star that appears after sunset, points the way. The caravan covers twenty-five miles a day, through a landscape void of landmarks. At night, the dromedaries kneel down in their caravan positions and are unloaded, hobbled, and carefully inspected to be sure the swaying movement of the pack saddle has not caused sores and that the soles of their hooves are in good condition. The camp's straight line arrangement facilitates departure the next morning. Six days later, the caravan arrives at the Fachi oasis, where it stops to restock

water, exchange information with other caravans, and do a bit of trading. From Fachi it is another five days to the Tree of Tenéré well. Then comes Tazolé, and finally Agadez. The long crossing is over. Not all caravans end at Agadez: many go on to the markets of northern Nigeria, where salt will be bartered for calico cloth dyed with indigo and sacks of millet. The Tuareg return to their camps in Air and the circle is completed until the next season. Time required: seventy to ninety days. Proceeds: buy at one and sell at fifteen, and time and effort don't count. The caravan is an exhausting, risky job: if it loses its way, the adventure could end in tragedy. The food is simple: millet porridge, milk, dates, and sweetened tea, providing no more than 1,500 calories a day. The Tuareg of the Hoggar undertake even longer voyages, traveling from the salt mines of Amadror to the Nigerian Sahel. In addition to salt, the caravans transport bales of dried medicinal plants, whose virtues are known and prized in southern villages. A single bag of these medicines is worth a load of millet. After getting the best possible prices, the caravans head back north; in addition to cereals, they carry wooden cooking utensils, dromedary saddles, sandals, veils dyed with indigo, and other wares that command good prices in the markets of the Hoggar. There are also much shorter routes around the salt mines of Teguidda-n-Tesemt, west of Agadez, in areas on the edge of the Sahara. The Kel Gress and other nomadic and seminomadic peoples of the Sahel supply the inhabitants of the area with millet, dried vegetables, earthenware jars, and squash bowls. In exchange, they receive salt and dates, cultivated in the palm groves of In Gall, not far from the mines. Some groups, like the Iberogan, Tuareg from the Tahoua region, trade in *taferkast*, the "salt earth" that covers the plains around Teguidda-n-Tesemt, about two hundred miles from their pasturelands. Taferkast costs nothing but the effort of collecting it. It is quite prized by herders, especially at the height of the dry season, when it is a vital food for the exhausted, malnourished herds. Aside from salt and its derivatives, transport in the Sahel region is now almost exclusively on wheels. Camels are used only to supply the most remote villages. The outcome of the silent battle between camel and truck is still in the balance. Trade by camel is the last thing protecting the lifestyle and identity of Sahara populations. *Azalai*, a word the Tuareg language uses for salt caravans, means "to part and then meet again," an exquisitely nomad concept that reminds us that one does not live in the desert. One passes through it.

256 A HERD FOLLOWS DUSTY ROADS IN THE VILLAGE OF TAMEGROUTE IN THE DRAA VALLEY. THE INHABITANTS OF SOUTHERN MOROCCO USE HERDING TO SUPPLEMENT RESOURCES FROM AGRICULTURE.

257 TOP LEFT SHEEP AND GOATS LIKE THIS HERD NEAR TOZEUR, TUNISIA, ARE PRECIOUS TO THE SAHARA NOMAD ECONOMY BECAUSE THEY CAN SUBSIST ON EVEN THE POOREST PASTURES.

PASTURELANDS

In the Sahara, it is the degree of mobility and the extent of movement possible that delimits pastureland, creating a map that reflects migratory routes, temporary or permanent springs and wells, vegetation in different places at various times of the year, places for restocking foodstuffs, and salt deposits. The annual cycle of moving from pasture to pasture in the desert is based on one key element: rain. Rainy and damp periods require endless travel from one pasture to the next, usually from south to north and back again. The extent of this movement depends on the distance between wet season and dry season pastures. The rainy season, which occurs in the summer, is a period of abundance. Grass is everywhere and water collects in pools and natural basins, freely available to the animals. It is the right time for "salt cures," when men and animals undertake long journeys to places known to be rich in mineral salts, which are vital to the health of the herds. In late winter, a dry period, the herders are forced to migrate south, where there is still a bit of poor pasture, gathering around the last spots of permanent water. For the Kababish of the northern Sudan, who are camel herders, how the land is used depends on a very exact calendar. During the hot, dry months, the Kababish gather along the dry rivers of the northern Kordofan, where there is water all year round, moving from one well to another in search of new pastures. The journeys back and forth are often long and exhausting. With the first rain in June, the tribes begin to move north, wandering from one pond to another, until October, which is the time of the *nugugh*, the great exodus toward the desert. Each group follows a clear path from which it cannot deviate, so as to leave enough grass for the return trip. When the pasture is exhausted in January, it is time for a rapid retreat to the wells in the south. The cycle ends until the next departure. In other cases, migratory movement is circular, generally for shorter dis-

257 TOP RIGHT THE LARGE THURSDAY MARKET ANIMATES THE TOWN OF DOUZ, TUNISIA. EXCHANGES OF LIVESTOCK AND PROVISIONS REQUIRE COMPLICATED NEGOTIATIONS THAT CAN GO ON FOR AN ENTIRE DAY.

257 BOTTOM IN TAMEGROUTE, LIKE ALL VILLAGES AND CAMPS IN THE SAHARA, HERDS RETURN FROM PASTURE BEFORE NIGHTFALL. ANIMALS OF MODEST VALUE, SHEEP AND GOATS ARE OFTEN CARED FOR BY CHILDREN.

258 LEFT AND RIGHT SHEEP AND GOATS ARE QUITE COMMON IN THE SAHARA, AS THEY CAN ENDURE PERSISTENT DROUGHTS AND MAKE MAXIMUM USE OF SCARCE DESERT PLANTS, EVEN FEEDING ON LEAVES AND SEEDLINGS STUBBORNLY PULLED FROM THORNY SHRUBS.

259 TOP THE DESERT NEAR CHINGUETTI, MAURITANIA, OFFERS VERY LITTLE EVEN FOR THE HIGHLY ADAPTABLE GOATS.

259 BOTTOM THE TUAREG OF AIR, IN NIGER, KNOW EXACTLY WHERE THE PERMANENT WATER HOLES ARE LOCATED; THESE ARE IMPORTANT STOPS DURING TRANSHUMANCE.

tances. The Kel Telataye, a Tuareg tribe from eastern Mali, make most of their movements during the rainy season, toward the salty lands of the north. Stops are brief, three or four days at the most. Movements are slower from November to January: the last grass available is used up as they gradually head south. Starting in February, the Kel Telataye settle near the wells around the village of Menaka, setting up their camps in the area for a couple of months, at a critical distance between pastures and watering

Some of the able-bodied men stay in the fields, while the others, usually the youngest, embark on the long journey north. The rhythm of the march is frenetic: in just a few weeks, the herds go back and forth across hundreds of miles, stopping at the salt deposits only as long as absolutely necessary. To maintain this speed, equipment must be reduced to a bare minimum. Anything that cannot be loaded onto a camel or a donkey is unnecessary. Tent dwellings, a symbol of the nomadic lifestyle, perfectly meet the requirements of this wandering existence. For nomads, a tent is more than shelter from desert adversities. It is a state of mind, a home for dreams and memories from which they may be absent for long periods, if survival requires it, but where they always return with joy. Tent size may vary depending on the wealth of the owner, but on average it is no larger than two hundred square feet. It is

holes. The arrival of the rains in July starts the whole process all over again. Groups that live in the more southern regions, where rainfall is more abundant, supplement their herding resources by growing a few grains, especially millet. As they must meet the needs of both the animals and the crops, seasonal movements must thus follow a dual calendar. Planting time at the start of the rainy season coincides with the obligatory departure in search of pastures. Similarly, if they want to be present for the harvest, the herders must return early. To accentuate the contradictions, agricultural areas are often quite far from the salt deposits: time works against the nomadic farmers. The richest tribes, like the Kel Gress in southern Nigeria, can count on the crops of a sufficient number of professional farmers, and can give up part of the planting. Less fortunate groups have only one choice: divide their forces.

rare to see a single tent: usually the camp is comprised of various tents, lined up or scattered across a relatively large area. A typical camp includes around fifteen tents belonging to different but closely related families. A tent can be raised anywhere, although in reality herders are creatures of habit and tend to return to the same place each year. During the rainy season, they prefer elevated, sandy places where water does not gather, while during the dry season they camp near trees that offer a bit of shade. The tent belongs to the woman; in the event of a divorce, she takes it with her, and the poor husband has no choice but to sleep out under the stars. The interior of the tent can be divided into different areas, with folding screens made of cloth or woven straw. Carpets or mats cover the sand-and-beaten-earth floor. The wooden bed, which consists of collapsible feet and posts, is

260 AND 261 For Sahara nomads, the tent in all its structural varieties is not only a shelter against the adversities of the desert climate, but above all a focal point where the family and social life of herders takes place.

262–263 Large camps like this one in the Algerian western Sahara, which have become increasingly rare, are set up only for important festivals and celebrations.

264–265 The interior of a tent may be sumptuous or more modest, depending on the owner's economic station, but carpets and mats always dominate.

the only important item of furniture, and is often adorned with blankets and decorated leather pillows. Food supplies are kept in leather sacks and bags hung from posts or arranged in a corner on the ground. Apart from this, tents are furnished with just a few other household items: utensils and cooking pots, a locked trunk for jewelry and other prized objects, goatskin water bags, terra-cotta jars for milk and butter, and saddles and harnesses. In the Sahara there are two basic types of tents, with endless variants and combinations, depending on the type of construction material available, and the surrounding environment. In the northern Sahara and Mauritania, where Arab influence was deep and lasting, the black tent of Bedouin origins predominates. It is used by the Chaamba, the Ouled Sliman, the Reguibat, the Tekna and the Arab-Berber tribes of Morocco and southern Algeria. The Kababish of Sudan use a similar model, but larger with a more complex structure, adapted to a more torrid climate. Tents used in the central part of the desert, including the Sahel area, are usually hemispherical; the Tuareg tent is a prototype of this style. The black tent consists of a goat or camel-wool cloth made up of several strips of fabric, one to two feet long and tightly stitched together. The canvas is held up by a framework of two or more wooden poles, joined at the top and resting

directly on the ground, which gives the black tent a typical cusp-like shape. The rope or leather stays are very long and tied to large wooden stakes. Low and rather small, but easy to set up and take down, the black tent is extremely practical, and requires only one dromedary to transport it.

Tuareg tents have a completely different construction style. The framework consists of a single central pole, supported by four other props on the sides, connected two by two with side bars. The cover is made of tanned goatskins, sewn together to form a geometric design: an average-size tent requires about sixty of them. Size depends on the family's wealth in animals: the Kel Dinnik of the Niger have been seen with tents made of 150 skins, enough for dozens of people. A common construction among the southern Tuareg includes parallel arches arranged like a portico: this structure is covered with mats woven with doum palm leaves or other plant material. This tent is also completely dismountable and transportable. It is more economical than a leather tent, and above all it is cooler and airier. In wool, leather, straw, or simply cotton, the tent is the thing that immediately identifies a herder's territory. Varying in size, this territory is meticulously divided into topographical sectors based on the landscape.

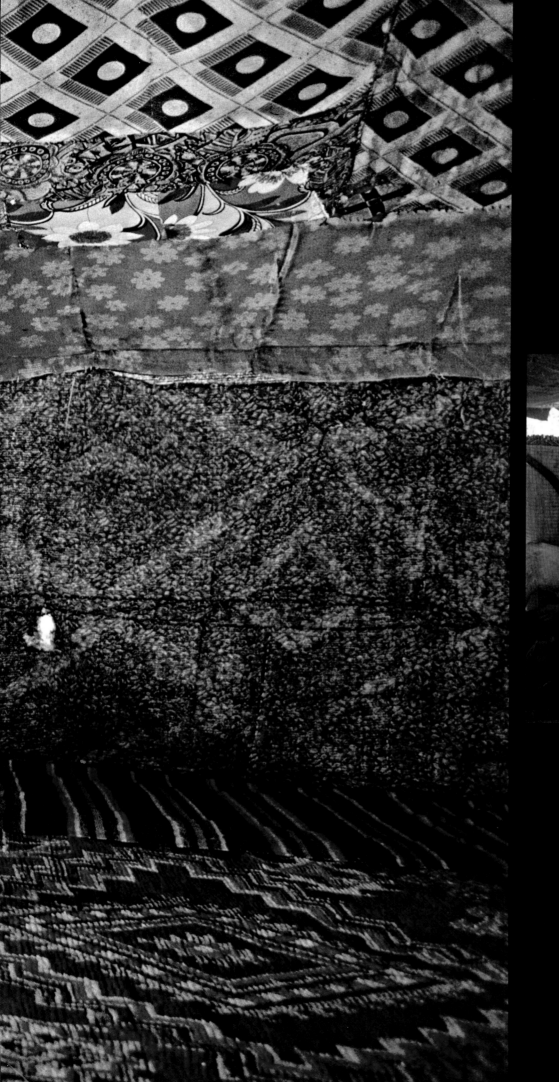

266 AND 267   This dwelling, used by the nomads of northern Chad, is one of the many versions of the hemispherical tent. The supporting skeleton is made of wooden poles, solidly joined to form a sort of arcade: this structure is difficult to replace in the desert, where large trees are rare, so it is jealously conserved as part of the family inheritance. The framework is then covered with mats made of plant material.

The nomads have extremely precise ways of perceiving their environment. Even places that seem to be void of landmarks and distinctive features can be inventoried. Sahara place names reveal the history of the people who live there, the available resources in a particular place, the identity of a route. In an elusive environment like the desert, a generic term is useless, at least with regard to what is important: water and vegetation. So details become almost feverishly precise. Water is life and its various names, associated with particular plants and trees, are the basis for many place names. The Tuareg distinguish endless types of water reserves, from puddles to artificial lakes. An *aguelman* is a natural basin among the rocks (*guelta* in Arabic); *tegidda* means

territorial border. Thus, Agadez is derived from the verb *egdez*, to visit, as a reminder of the close but sporadic relationship the nomadic tribes of the Air have with their capital. For the Tuareg of Mali, the Gourma region past the Niger is Harabanda, literally "beyond the water": another country where desert men are strangers. The nomadic areas of the various clans are thus delimited by invisible coordinates that establish how water and plant resources will be used. On this virtual map, some places have a special meaning, becoming landmarks in both space and time. Frequented since ancient times, for nomads they are fixed gathering places around which the group identity takes shape as they revisit their common past. The need for spiritual appropriation of territory is especially acute in the Sahara, where the landscape tolerates no lasting testimony of human society. So in Taouardei in the Mali Sahara, rock carvings and tombs of mythical ancestors certify the sacredness of the site, which becomes a temple of collective memory. Recent studies found a series of elements in Taouardei that reveal

a bowl-shaped cavity full of rainwater; *aguel hok* means small valley (the name of a village in the Tilemsi in Mali); *anu* means deep well; *ibankar* means a shallower well; *fonfu* is a pumping facility; *ersan* means holes carved in the sandy bed of a wadi. As a result, *Tegidda-n-tesemt* means salty water; *Tegidda-n-tageyt* means doum palm wells; *Ibankar-n-iklan* is a servants' well; *Anu-n-agerof* is a (deep) well of *Tribulus terrestris*, a thorny herb; *Agel-man-n-tamat* is the water basin of the tamat acacia (*A. ehrenber-giana*). Other place names refer to acts of daily life, wild animals, and parts of the human body. In certain cases, the name of a place marks a memorable date, a past event, or even delimits a

the symbolic and functional role of the area: next to permanent wells, which are absolutely necessary for the herders and their animals, are areas used as a cemetery and a mosque, nothing more than a circle of rocks in the sand. Farther off, a pile of granite boulders is identified as a home of the ancestors. Nearby, a heavy slab of rock probably served as a lithophone. Taouardei is still a vital node in nomadic culture: it is no coincidence that in 1992, this is where negotiations began between the leaders of the Tuareg rebellion and the government representatives of Mali. In the Sahara, history keeps passing through the same places.

270 Plastic drums, which have been a part of the nomads' material culture for some time, are for this Sudanese herder a reliable complement to his goatskin bags.

271 As new wells are dug under the auspices of international aid organizations, the lives of Sudanese herders have become less difficult, but this has often triggered desertification and irreversible environmental deterioration.

272–273 A group of Tuareg from Niger is busy digging an open well. It may require weeks of collective work to reach the underground water table, which is often quite deep.

274 AND 275 TOP LEFT THE STATE OF ABANDON OF THE STREETS OF OUALATA,
MAURITANIA, CONTRASTS WITH THE ATTRACTIVE DECORATIONS THAT ADORN ITS DWELLINGS.

275 TOP RIGHT AND 275 BOTTOM A TYPICAL RIVER BOAT SLIDES ALONG THE
WATERS OF THE NIGER (TOP RIGHT). THE MOSQUE IN DJENNÉ (BOTTOM) GIVES AN IDEA OF
THE ANCIENT SPLENDOR OF SAHARA CITIES.

276–277 THE VILLAGE OF TIMIMOUN, AT THE EDGES OF THE ALGERIAN TUAT,
IS DOMINATED BY THE RUINS OF THE FORTRESS, NOW ALMOST INDISTINGUISHABLE
FROM THE ERODED HILLS SURROUNDING IT.

DESERT
CAPITALS

The relationship with surrounding regions was what defined the nature of the city: it was an impenetrable core folded in on itself, but at the same time its opposite, a door open to contact with strangers and outside influences. The cities that sprang up on the two shores of the desert had to act as caravan ports of call that gathered and concentrated goods from everywhere. The great capitals that arose on the northern shore of the Sahara, like Sigilmassa, Tahert, and Sedrata, were surrounded by fortified walls, yet were first and foremost important trading centers. To the south, this tendency was even more evident. Decadent but pulsing with life, even today Timbuktu, Gao, and Agadez farther west retain the features of commercial caravan cities they inherited from a not too distant past. Of the cities of the Maghreb, stretching out in a parallel line along the Atlas range, nothing remains but ruins. The most famous, Sigilmassa, was in southern Morocco near present-day Rissani. In Europe, the city was known as the main intersection for traffic to the African kingdoms of the South, where gold was abundant. Merchants from all over the Islamic world established trading bases in Sigilmassa, which became one of the most important mints in the Almoravide empire. Founded in the eighth century by Arab-Berber groups, the city played a dominant role until its destruction in the second half of the fourteenth century by a mysterious nomadic tribe from the south. The

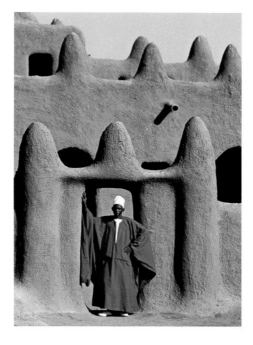

southern terminal of the trans-Sahara route that left from Sigilmassa, the city of Aoudaghost lies in rubble among the sands of Mauritania, south of the Tichitt fault. It is believed that the city had at least three thousand inhabitants, a number that could double with the arrival of the great caravans. The Almoravide conquest around 1050 permanently erased Aoudaghost from the map of trans-Sahara trade. Thirty years later, Kumbi Saleh, the capital of Ghana, was sacked, and the kingdom began a slow decline. The subsequent rise of a new empire, Mali, shifted the center of traffic to the west and the bend of the Niger. The cities of Oualata, Timbuktu, and Gao became the new fulcrums of inter-African trade. Oualata, located in the Hodh region of Mauritania, is now a sleepy, half-abandoned town. The small, cube-shaped houses are embellished with decorations and relief work that adorn the entry gates and walls of the dwellings, with designs that symbolize parts of the human body with the sinuous appearance of Arabic script. The city, which until 1700 rivaled Timbuktu in wealth and culture, now has no more than three hundred inhabitants. Its decline was rapid, almost immediate. The beginning of the slave trade and the consequent opening of new trading routes to the ocean were fatal to many Sahara cities. Only Agadez and the towns along the Niger were able to survive the change imposed by the new international situation.

278–279 THE COMMERCIAL GOOD FORTUNE OF DJENNÉ, WHICH REACHED ITS HEIGHT IN THE SIXTEENTH CENTURY, WAS DUE PRIMARILY TO ITS GEOGRAPHICAL POSITION, WHICH ALLOWED THE CITY TO BENEFIT FROM TRANS-SAHARA TRAFFIC AND AT THE SAME TIME GAIN ACCESS TO THE AGRICULTURAL AND MINERAL RESOURCES OF BLACK AFRICA.

280–281 WITH THE MAGNIFICENCE OF A MEDIEVAL CATHEDRAL, THE GREAT MOSQUE OF DJENNÉ OVERLOOKS THE TOWN CENTER. THE EDIFICE, DESTROYED DURING THE HOLY WAR UNLEASHED BY CHEIKOU AMADOU IN 1830, WAS REBUILT IN 1907. SUPPORTED BY NINETY LARGE PILLARS, IT IS ONE OF THE MOST IMPORTANT MUD-BRICK MONUMENTS IN THE WORLD.

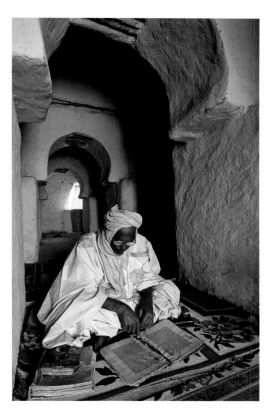

282 AND 283 OUALATA, ONCE SO
PROSPEROUS THAT IT RIVALED
TIMBUKTU IN WEALTH, CONCEALS
UNEXPECTED TREASURES: HUNDREDS
OF BOOKS, MANUSCRIPTS, AND
TREATISES ON HISTORY, GEOMETRY,
AND ASTRONOMY, CAREFULLY
CONSERVED IN THE MOST SHELTERED
AREAS OF PUBLIC AND PRIVATE
EDIFICES. MOST OF THESE WORKS HAVE
NOT YET BEEN CATALOGUED.

284 TOP Many houses in Timbuktu are built of clay bricks pressed into special molds and dried in the sun.

284 BOTTOM The architecture of Timbuktu is quite simple: seen from above, its edifices look austere and plain.

285 TOP LEFT The Tuareg, whose camps surround the edge of the city, controlled Timbuktu many times in the past.

285 TOP RIGHT Although the population of Timbuktu has been reduced to a few thousand inhabitants, the city still has an open, cosmopolitan air.

285 BOTTOM The design of the Djinguereber mosque, the oldest in Timbuktu, is said to resemble a man in a position of prayer.

TIMBUKTU, THE CAPITAL OF LEGENDS

The inland Niger delta was a system whose various elements were connected by a design that was both symbolic and practical. In an anthropomorphic representation dear to African tradition, Timbuktu was the head of an immense figure whose feet rested on the salt mines of Teghazza and Taoudeni. The river joined it to Djennè, the belly, where resources where concentrated and processed. San, Sofara, and Mopti, secondary ports, were the neck and limbs, the open hands that gathered goods from the myriad canals of the delta. In this sort of primal global village, Timbuktu played the role of cultural and religious guarantor. Legend states that the city was founded in 1100, at a well guarded by a Berber slave named Bunctù, the "Great Mother." Its position, between the river and the desert, made it an ideal place for trading and contact. It was a double port, with caravans arriving from the roads of the Sahara and great pirogues sailing in loaded with products from the south. Timbuktu was connected to all terminals in the northern Sahara, and through Agadez to Lake Chad and Egypt. The ethnic composition of the city's population fully reflected this colossal network of relationships: Berbers, Arabs, Moroccans, natives of Tripoli, Moors from Spain, Mossi, Haoussa, Mande, and Songhai all lived in or frequently visited Timbuktu in a climate of reciprocal tolerance. In the sixteenth century, Timbuktu had 100,000 inhabitants, compared to barely 20,000 today. At the same time, it was a cosmopolitan business city, a holy place and above all a city of wise men. The university, where scholars from all areas of Islam studied, taught not only religion, but also music, astronomy, geometry, and law. Seen from above, the city looks like a uniform expanse of rectangular, grayish brown houses. The three mosques of Timbuktu, Djinguereber, Sankoré, and Sidi Yaya are the oldest in the Sudan region. Djinguereber, whose design resembles a man in a praying position, was built in the first half of the fourteenth century, although it appears that the original core of the structure is even older. The prayer rooms, whose ceilings are supported by uniform rows of pillars, are arranged next to a large open courtyard reserved for women. On the north side is a square mud-brick minaret, whose structure is strengthened by a framework of wooden beams protruding from the surface, which also serve as a scaffolding for any repairs. The mosque of Sankoré, a century younger than Djinguereber and once the site of a famous university school, has a similar structure. Sidi Yaya, the third religious center of Timbuktu, is dedicated to one of the most honored historical figures of the city.

Nearby are the houses where the first European explorers stayed: Laing, the Englishman; Caillé, the Frenchman; and Barth, the German. Laing was killed on his way back, but Caillé and Barth returned home to speak of their disappointment. The Timbuktu they saw was a far cry from the splendor of the past, and the caravans from Morocco and Libya traveled there ever less frequently. Yet Barth observed that

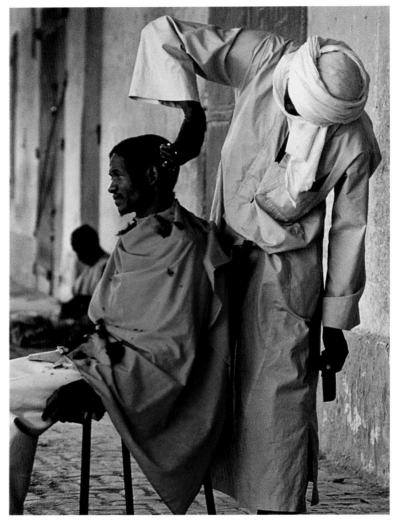

286 **RIGHT** Like modern shopping centers, the business districts of southern Sahara cities offer not only goods but services.

287 Timbuktu has large, distinctive city vegetable gardens, located on terraces that descend in concentric circles toward the well.

288 **AND** 289 Massive Moorish-style wooden doors, adorned with studs and wrought-iron decoration, look out over the intricate streets of Timbuktu.

290–291 The indoor market of Timbuktu sells vegetables, cereals, dried fish, dates, and, of course, the precious salt of Taoudeni.

in the mid-1800s a significant amount of gold still traveled the road to Ghadames and Tripoli, while Malabar silk and red cloth, produced in Saxony, came from Kano. From the southern savannas came large quantities of rice and grains, vegetable butter, and cotton. The caravans from the north brought Manchester calico and English razors; eyeglasses from Nuremberg; tobacco and dates from Tuat; Arabian mantles and shawls from Tunis; fretwork windows; and sugar and tea from Morocco. But the soul of trade, then as now, was the salt of Taoudeni. In 1980, 7,500 tons of salt were traded on the square of Timbuktu for the equivalent of about 1 million dollars: a vital contribution to the city's economy. As in the past, the salt

caravans stop at the gates of the city, and business transactions are concluded in private homes, while the market sells primarily staple products. Timbuktu conceals the last of its secrets, thousands of ancient books and manuscripts, within studded trunks in gray, shadowy stone houses and the tents of nomads camped outside the city. The manuscripts are for the most part historical and geographical treatises, unusual chronicles that can be studied to perhaps reveal many shadowy aspects of the Sahara and African past. Since 1977, a research center directed by a council of city wise men has been working on collecting and classifying documents scattered over a vast area of the Mali Sahara.

292 LEFT THE ASKIA MAUSOLEUM IN GAO IS A TYPICAL SAHARA STRUCTURE, MADE OF COMMON MUD BRICKS AND THE MUCH RARER WOOD.

292 CENTER AND RIGHT AND 293 THE GREAT MOSQUE OF AGADEZ IS DOMINATED BY A PYRAMID-SHAPED MINARET, STABILIZED WITH POLES SET INTO THE EARTHEN WALLS (CENTER). THE BUILDINGS OF AGADEZ HAVE THICK WALLS OF MUD BRICKS, WHICH ARE MADE FROM A MIXTURE OF CLAY, WATER, AND CUT STRAW.

294–295 THE TAMALAKOYE MARKET IN AGADEZ OFFERS GOODS OF EVERY TYPE, AS WELL AS THE CHANCE TO SOCIALIZE, WHICH IS FUNDAMENTAL FOR DESERT PEOPLES.

GAO AND AGADEZ

After flowing past Timbuktu, the Niger continues its course eastward, to the city of Gao. Little more than a village when Timbuktu was in its heyday, Gao owed its fortune to the emergence of Songhai power in the second half of the fifteenth century. The new kingdom, which extended from the Atlantic to the Air Mountains, made Gao its new trading and political capital. Rich, cosmopolitan, and powerful, Gao once counted over seventy thousand inhabitants. Connected to all the great trans-Saharan roads, the city became the favorite terminal for routes leading to the markets of the central and eastern Sahara. The vestiges of Gao's illustrious past include the ruins of an ancient mosque and the Askia Mausoleum, marking the dynasty that controlled the fortunes of Songhai until the Moroccan conquest in 1591. Built in the sixteenth century, it looks like a truncated pyramid about forty feet high, bristling with contorted branches that seem to naturally rise from the floor. Gao is now a city in slow, inexorable decline.

Agadez has met a far better fate. It is the only city that seems to have been spared the more or less marked decadence that has struck all the great cities of the southern Sahara. According to oral tradition, Agadez was founded in the sixteenth century by the son of the sultan of Istanbul, Younus, who had been asked by a group of Tuareg nobles to end the anarchy that was afflicting the region. Even today, the sultan of Agadez is by tradition an "outsider" who is usually selected from the black population: he may marry a Tuareg woman, but his children may not suc-

ceed him in office. Located at the intersection of the roads that linked the southern countries to Egypt and the Libyan and Algerian oases, the city experienced a long period of prosperity. Surrounded by walls, it had a population of about fifty thousand inhabitants, most of whom were artisans dedicated to metal and leather work. This production base, which was lacking in Timbuktu, allowed Agadez to overcome difficult times in its history and retain its role as regional capital up to the present. The old city is divided into eleven districts, each with its mosque. The groups of houses, often two stories high, are separated by a maze of lanes wide enough for donkeys and dromedaries to pass with their loads. The Tamalakoye market has always been the fulcrum of Agadez: lively at any time of day, it is not only a trading area, but a true shopping center that offers goods as well as a vast array of services. Alongside the shops and grocery stores are restaurants, barber shops, mechanics, bicycle rentals, mills, tailors, and shoemakers. Not far off, the immense yet graceful Great Friday Mosque dominates the entire city. Built in 1500, its original features are still intact today. The minaret, in pure Sudanese style, is eighty-eight feet tall: the contrast with the prayer room, unadorned and with a ceiling so low that one can barely stand upright, is absolutely spectacular. An expression of the power of the sultanate, the Friday Mosque is a symbol of Agadez and its dominant role in the region. After a difficult period the city managed to reinvent itself; once a caravan gathering place, it has now become a junction point, a vital stop for people and goods moving from North Africa to countries south of the Sahara. Commerce is expanding: there are hundreds of registered businesses plus thousands of anonymous transactions that take place among rural populations every day. Handicrafts and agriculture at the foot of the Air Mountains are flourishing more than ever. Agadez has learned how to blend tradition and modernity, reviving its ancient vocation as a market city and great crossroads of the Sahara.

INDEX

Note   *c = caption*

A

Abd el Melik, 53
Abdallahi, 36
Acacus, see Tradrart Acacus
Addax nasomaculatus, 127
Adrar, 70, 106
Africa, 11, 22, 25, 26, 29, 29c, 32,
    35, 39, 39d, 43, 44, 48, 54, 61,
    62, 105, 127, 137, 138, 141,
    154, 198c, 218, 241, 242, 278c,
    292
Agadez, 39, 48, 108, 156, 166c, 218,
    242, 242c, 248, 268, 275, 285,
    292c
Aguelman, 268
Ahmed Baba, 39
Ahnet, 106, 107
Aïr, 14d, 39, 48, 62, 108, 141, 141c,
    156, 166c, 182c, 226d, 242, 248,
    258c, 268, 292
Alcazar-Quivir, battle of 31c
Alexander the Great, 32
Algeria, 8c, 13, 13c, 40, 44, 46, 54,
    65, 70, 73, 88c, 105, 108, 137,
    137c, 138, 141, 154, 198, 225, 229,
    261
Algiers, 13, 40
Alì, sovereign of the Uadai, 43
Allah, 53, 56, 70, 156
Al-Mansur, 31, 31c
Almasy, Laszlo, 53
Amadror, 45, 106, 242, 248
Andalusia, 241
Aoudaghost, 26, 275
Aoulef, 73
Arak Gorges, 70
Araouane, 36, 81c 194
Archei Gorge, 105c, 108, 112c
Archenti Mountains, 52
Aristida pungens, 119
Arlit, 166c, 229
Askia, 292, 292c;
    Mohammed, 31
Assekrem, 62, 106
Asyut, 40d
Atakor, 62, 105, 106, 106c, 107,
    154
Atar, 70

Atarantes, 153
Atlantic Ocean, 14, 30c, 32, 44, 65,
    69, 70c, 76c, 292
Atlas (mountain range), 26c, 40, 62,
    88c, 108, 154, 163c, 226, 226c,
    275
Audouin-Dubreil, Louis, 54, 54c,
    56c
Auenat Mountains, 52, 53
Augiéras, 53
Augila oasis, 32
Augilae, 153
Azaouak, valley of, 62
Azger, Tuareg, 36, 40, 45, 49, 72c
Azizia, 73

B

Badaire, 47
Baghirmi, 35, 43
Bagzane mountains, 108
Bahr el-Ghazal, 108
Bandiagara, 142
Barberia, 29, 30
Bardai, 107
Barth, Heinrich, 39, 39c, 44, 285
Baussy, 50
Bedo, 242
Beja, 198
Belèd-es-Sudàn, 26, 29, 31, 241
Beni Isguen, 198
Benué River, 40
Berabich, 242c
Berbers, 154, 285
Bideyat, 108, 191, 191c
Bilma, 35, 70, 242, 242c, 248c
Biskra, 45, 53
Blue Nile, 62
Bojador, Cape 50
Bokou, lake, 83c
Bonaparte, Napoleon, 32
Bornu, 32, 35, 39c, 40, 42c, 43, 191
Bororo, 201, 201c, 203c, 205c,
    209c
Bou Noura, 198
Bubalus antiquus, 142
Bushmen, 142

C

Cabili, 154
Cabra, 36, 44, 47

Caillé, René, 36, 36c, 39c, 44, 46,
    285
Cairo, 32, 62, 242
Cameroon, 191c
Canary Islands, 46, 50
Canis aureus, 127
Cape Town, 53
Caracal caracal, 128c
Carthage, 25
Caspian Sea, 61, 69
Cerastes cerastes, 124
Chaamba, 153, 198, 261
Chad, 14c, 39, 48, 56, 61c, 62,
    69, 70, 83, 107, 144c, 191,
    191c, 198, 198c, 218c, 242,
    267c
Chad, Lake, 32, 35, 35c, 47, 49,
    49c, 61c, 62, 69, 76c, 108, 112c,
    237c, 242, 285
Cheikou Amadou, 278c
Chinguetti, 228c, 258c
Chiriet, 241c
Citrullus colocynthis, 119, 121c
Clapperton, Hugh, 35, 35c
Congo, 48
Cornelius Balbo, 25
Cufra, 40, 52, 52c, 53, 70
Cyrenaica, 22, 49, 52
Cyrene, 25

D

Dahkla, 40d
Dakar, 53
Danthonia, 119
Darfur, 43, 191, 242
Dead Sea, 83c
Dei, Benedetto, 29
Démi, 242
Denham, Dixon, 35, 35c
Dhar Oualata, 228c
Djado, 76c, 106c, 225
Djanet, 49, 70c, 106, 137c, 144c,
    153c, 229, 241, 242
Djenné, 36, 47, 275c, 278c, 285
Djinguereber, 285
Djouf, 194
Dogon, 142
Domitian, 25
Douls, Camille, 46, 51
Douz, 257c

Draa Valley, 257c
Duveyrer, Henri, 40, 45, 47

E

Egeré, 45
Egypt, 8c, 22, 32, 36, 40, 40c, 52, 62,
    65c, 70, 99c, 138c, 149, 228c, 285,
    292
Ek Glessour, 11c
El-Atteuf, 198
El-Faiyum, oasis 62c, 228c
El-Golea, 40, 47, 198
El-Hasan ibn Muhammad
    el Wazzan, 29
El-Kharga, oasis, 40c, 70
El-Kraer-Hadgi, 44
Eliaziz, 46
Elmina, 29
Emi Koussi, 62, 107
Ennedi, 52, 62, 105d, 108, 108c,
    112d, 127, 141, 149, 191, 191c
Erg Chech, 62, 70
Ethiopia, 40
Ethiopians, 153

F

Fachi, 242, 242c, 244c, 248c
Fada, 112c
Fadnoun plateau, 156
Faya, 70
Fennecus zerda, 124c, 127
Fez, 36, 241
Fezzan, 22, 25, 32, 32c, 35, 39, 40,
    43, 47, 52, 84c, 137, 141c, 218c,
    228c, 242
Flatters, Paul, 45, 45c, 47, 48
Forbes, Rosita, 52, 52c
Foucault, Charles de, 52c, 53
Foureau, Fernand, 46, 47, 48
France, 36, 44, 45c, 48, 49, 53, 56
Freudenberg, Josef, 32
Fulani (see also Peul), 44

G

Gadafouà, 69
Gaetulians, 153
Gafsa, oasis, 138
Gambia, 31
Gao, 29, 31, 39, 70, 241, 242, 275,
    292, 292c

Garamantes, 22, 25
Garet el-Djenoun, 106
Gazella dorcas, 127c
Gebel Indinen, 61c
Ghadames, 36, 40, 52, 154, 187c,
    229, 237c, 241, 285
Ghana, 26, 29, 275
Ghardaia, 198
Ghat, 40, 49, 52, 99c, 241
Giarabub, 52
Gilf Kebir, 53, 61c
Giza, 228c
Gourara, 228
Gourma, 268
Granada, 29
Great Eastern Erg, 46, 62, 228
Great Lakes, 62
Great Western Erg, 62, 226
Gréboun, Mount, 108
Grévy, 44
Guinea, 26
Guinea, Gulf of, 29, 32, 35c, 45
Guir, Hammada del, 226

H

Haardt Gorge-Marie, 54c
Habeter, 142
Haoussa, 35, 242, 285
Harabanda, 261
Hassanein, Ahmed Mohamed bey, 52,
    52c,
Hassi Messaoud, 229
Herodotus, 22
Hirafok, 107
Hodh, 275
Hoggar, 14, 26, 36, 40, 45, 45c, 48,
    49, 52c, 53, 62, 65, 70, 73, 105,
    105c, 106, 106c, 107, 141, 154,
    241, 248
Holland, 50
Hornemann, Friedrich, 32
Houghton, 32
Husein Kemal-el-Din, 53

I

Ibn Battuta, 26
Ibrahim, 46
Idelès, 107
Idjil, 242
Iforhas, 106

Iheren, 149
Ilaman, 49, 106
Imilchil, 163c
Imraguen, 194
In Gall, 178c, 180c
In Salah, 36, 49c, 70
Izerguil, 50

J

Jabbaren, 141
Joffre, 47
Juby, Cape, 50
Jupiter Ammon, 32

K

Kababish, 257, 261
Kalahari, 141
Kanasai Valley, 106c
Kanem, 43, 191
Kano, 242, 286
Kanuri, 244
Katsina, 242
Kawar, 76c, 191, 242
Kel (Tuareg tribe):
    Ajjar, 154;
    Dinnik, 261;
    Gress, 156, 248, 258;
    Hoggar, 154;
    Iforhas, 156;
    Telataye, 258;
    Timbuktu, 156
Kenya, 142
Khartoum, 43
Kordofan, 257
Kuka, 39, 43
Kumbi Saleh, 275
Kusseri, 48

L

Lagos, 40
Laing, Alexander Gordon, 36, 39, 40,
    285
Lamy, 48
Laouni, 11
Laperrine d'Hautpoul, Joseph, 52, 53,
    54
Las Palmas, 50
Lebaudy, Jacques, 50, 51, 51c
Ledyard, John, 32, 45c
Leo Africanus, 29, 30

Leo X, 29
Leptis Magna, 25
Libya, 8d, 22, 22c, 52, 54, 56, 61,
    61c, 62, 70, 73, 106c, 110c, 127c,
    141, 142, 144c, 154, 187c, 218c,
    237, 241, 285
Libyan Desert, 62, 65c, 70, 137,
    242
Libyans, 22
Logoné River, 62
Lucas, William, 32
Lyon, Gorge Francis, 32, 32c

M

Ma el-Ainin, 46, 50c, 51
Maghreb, 29, 46, 275
Magone, 25
Malabar, 286
Malfante, Antonio, 29
Mali, 13c, 26, 81c, 154, 156,
    218c, 242, 242c, 247c, 258, 268,
    275
Manchester, 286
Mande, 285
Mohammed, 46
Moroccans, 285
Morocco, 13c, 25, 29, 31, 32, 36,
    40, 44, 50, 51, 52, 56, 108, 156c,
    226c, 241, 257c, 261, 275, 285,
    286
Marrakech, 31, 46, 161c, 163c,
    241
Mattata, 218c
Mauri, 36, 46, 50, 50c, 51, 56,
    153c, 156c, 194, 194c,
    198
Mauritania, 11c, 51, 70, 70c, 73c,
    76c, 127c, 153c, 154, 194,
    218c, 228c, 229, 241, 242,
    247c, 258c, 261, 268c, 275,
    275c
Mecca, 47, 138c, 286c
Mediterranean Sea, 45c, 61, 62, 69,
    154, 218
Melika, 198
Menaka, 258
Mertoutek, 107
Mina, 26c
Mogador, 51
Monod, Théodore, 53

Mountain of Embalmed Corpses,
    32
Monteil, 47
Montes Claros (Atlas), 26c
Mopti, 285
Mori, 285
Mossi, 285
Mourdi, 108
Mouydir, 106, 107
Mozabites, 153, 154, 198
Muhammad ibn Abdallah al-Lawati,
    26
Murzuk, 32, 32c, 35, 43, 70, 84c,
    241
Mussa Ag Amastan, 49
Mzab, 40, 198, 229

N

Nabta Playa, 138c
Nachtigal, Gustav, 42c, 43, 43c
Napoleon III, 40
Nasamons, 22, 153
Near East, 29, 53
Niamey, 62
Niger, 11, 201, 225c, 226c, 229, 241c,
    242, 258, 261, 271
Niger River, 31, 32, 39, 40, 44,
    47, 47c, 62, 65, 81c, 156, 198c,
    218, 241, 242, 248c, 275, 275c,
    285, 292
Nigeria, 35c, 201, 248
Nile, 29, 40c, 43, 52, 61, 62, 62c,
    138, 153, 218, 242
Nile Valley, 191, 198
Niola Doa, 144c
North Africa, 11, 25, 25c, 138,
    154
Noun, Cape, 50
Numidians, 153

O

Oea, 25
Okiek, 142
Omar, sultan of Bornu, 43
Ouadane, 241
Oualata, 194, 228c, 241, 275, 275c,
    283c
Ouargla, 45, 48, 53, 198, 229
Oubanghi-Chari, 56c
Oundney, Walter, 34c, 35, 35c

Ouled Sliman, 261
Ounianga Kebir, 83c
Ounianga Serir, 14c, 83c
Overweg, Adolf, 39, 39c

P
Park, Mungo, 32
Persia, 30, 228
Peul, 153, 198, 198c
Phazania (Fezzan), 25
Picco Toussidé, 107
Polo, Marco, 29
Pompeii, 22c
Portugal, 31

Q
Qattara Depression, 62, 62c

R
Rabah, 48, 49c
Ramusio, 29
Red Sea, 65, 198
Reggane, 70
Reguibat, 194, 261
Remelé, Philippe, 40c
Richardson, James, 39, 39c
Río de Oro, 52, 56
Ritchie, Joseph, 32, 32c
Rohlfs, Gerhard, 40, 40c
Rwanda, 142

S
Sabratha, 25
Sahel, 13, 56, 70, 73c, 137, 154, 242, 248
Saint-Louis, 44, 47
Salah, 48
Salisbury, Robert Cecil, lord, 47
Samburu, 142
San, 141, 285
Sankoré, 285, 286c
Sebastian, king of Portugal, 31
Sebcha, 45
Sebfia, oasis, 218c
Sefar, 149, 149c
Séguedine, 242
Seguiet el-Hamra, 51
Senegal, 31, 44, 198, 198c, 247c

Senegal River, 65, 76c, 218
Senussi, 40, 52, 53
Si El-Hadgi Abd-el-Kader, 44
Sidi Yaya, 285
Sierra Leone, 36
Sijilmassa, 26, 29, 241, 275
Sinai Peninsula, 61c, 62c
Sissé, spires of, 107
Siwa, oasis, 32, 40, 237c, 242
Smara, 50c, 51
Soborom, 107, 248
Sofara, 285
Sokoto, 35c
Sollum, 52
Songhai, 31, 285, 292
Souf, 228c, 229
Stenodactylus petriei, 128c
Strabo, 225c
South Africa, 142
Sudan, 11, 26, 61c, 108, 257, 261, 271c
Sudd, 62
Suez, 47
Suez, Gulf of, 62
Sus, 46

T
Tademait, 48
Tadrart Acacus, 8d, 14, 61c, 69c, 72c, 73c, 84c, 88c, 99c, 106c, 149, 149c
Tafassasset, 106c
Tafilalet, oasis, 40
Tahat, 106
Tahert, 275
Tahoua, 248
Tamanrasset, 52, 70, 73c, 106, 106c
Tamegrout, 257c
Tamerza, 225c
Tamrit, 112c
Tanezrouft, 36, 53, 105, 107
Tangiers, 26, 36, 40
Taouardei, 268
Taoudeni, 241, 242, 242c, 247c, 285, 286, 286c
Tassili n-Ajjer, 22c, 49, 62, 65, 99c, 105, 106, 107, 112c, 149c, 154, 198

Tazolé, 248
Tazrouk, 107
Tebu, 22, 35, 153, 191, 191c, 194
Teda, 107
Teffedest, 106
Teghaza, 30, 31, 241, 242, 285
Teguedei, oasis, 218c
Teguidda-n-Tesemt, 248
Teguiddam Tessoum, 242
Tekna, 261
Telertheba, 106
Tenere, 70, 76c, 105, 106c, 108, 127c, 137c, 138c, 191, 229, 241c, 242c
Terarart, 144c
Terkei, 149c
Tibesti, 14, 22, 35, 42c, 43, 52, 61c, 62, 65, 69, 70, 105, 105c, 107, 108, 110c, 191, 191c, 248c
Tichitt, oasis, 228c, 241, 242, 275
Tidikelt, 48, 154
Tilemsi, 268
Tim Missao, 106
Timbuktu, 11, 29, 31, 32, 32c, 36, 36c, 39, 39c, 40, 44, 45c, 47, 47c, 50, 53, 54, 166c, 218, 218c, 241, 242c, 247c, 275, 283c, 285, 285c, 286, 286c, 292
Timimoun, 73, 22c, 228, 275c
Timiris, Cape, 194
Tin Hinan, 156
Tin Reroh, 106, 107
Tin Tazarift, 198
Tin Zuaten, oasis, 53
Tisemt, 106
Tissoukai, 198
Tit, 49
Togo, 43
Tombutto, 30
Touggourt, 54, 54c, 229
Tozeur, 257c
Tripoli, 31, 32, 32c, 35, 36, 39, 39c, 40, 43, 47, 237c, 241, 242, 285
Tripolitania, 49, 52, 191
Troglodytes, 153
Tropic of Cancer, 105, 242

Trou au Natron, 191
Tuareg (see also Azger and Kel), 8c, 13, 13c, 14c, 26, 29, 30, 31, 31c, 32, 32c, 39, 44, 45, 45c, 46c, 47, 47c, 48, 49, 49c, 54, 106, 153, 154, 154c, 156, 156c, 166c, 173c, 187c, 191, 194, 194c, 198, 209c, 242, 244c, 248, 258c, 261, 268, 271, 285c, 292
Tuat, 40, 70, 154, 225, 226, 241, 286
Tummo, 43
Tunis, 25c, 31, 43, 241, 286
Tunisia, 25c, 43, 44, 218c, 228c, 257c
Turkey, 53
Tutsi, 142

U
Uadai, 35, 43, 39
Uan Derbaouen, 198

V
Valpreda, Giuseppe, 43
Varanus griseus, 127c
Vieuchange, Michel, 52, 52c
Vogel, Eduard, 39, 39c, 43

W
Wadi Djerat, 22c
Wadi Draa, 40, 226c
Wadi Halfa, 11
Wadi Mathandous, 72, 88c, 141, 142c, 144c
Wadi Tafassasset, 106
Wadi Tin Tarabin, 106

X
Xhosa, 142

Y
Yoa, Lake, 83
Younus, 292
Ysalguier, Anselmo di, 29

Z
Zanzibar, 39, 43
Zarzura, oasis, 52, 53
Zinder, 48

PHOTO CREDITS

ACKNOWLEDGMENTS

I would like to thank some of the many people who assisted, aided, and encouraged me in writing this book. Alberto Salza, anthropologist and companion on African travels, wrote the introduction. Enrico Guasco and Evasio Anrò helped me reread the drafts. The Centre de Documentation et de Recherches "Ahmed Baba" in Timbuktu gave me a warm reception and is now doing invaluable work in recovering documents and ancient manuscripts in the Mali Sahara. I am grateful to all of you.

Paolo Novaresio

TRANSLATION

Studio Traduzione Vecchia, Milan

300 A GIGANTIC SWATHE OF DUNES STRETCHES OUT ACROSS THE PLAIN OF
COMPACT SEDIMENTS IN THE DESOLATE LIBYAN SAHARA. DURING THE SUMMER,
FROM EARLY JUNE TO LATE AUGUST, IT WOULD BE IMPOSSIBLE TO WALK BAREFOOT
ON THE INVITING SAND, WHICH UNDER THE BLAZING SUN CAN REACH
TEMPERATURES APPROACHING 160°F.

Thunder Bay Press
An imprint of the Advantage Publishers Group
5880 Oberlin Drive, San Diego, CA 92121-4794
www.thunderbaybooks.com

Copyright © 2003 White Star S.r.l.

All notations of errors or omissions
should be addressed to Thunder Bay
Press, Editorial Department, at the
address at left. All other correspondence
(author inquiries, permissions)
concerning the content of this book
should be addressed to White Star S.r.l.,
Via C. Sassone, 22/24, 13100 Vercelli,
Italy, www.whitestar.it.

ISBN 1-59223-038-5

Printed in Italy
1 2 3 4 5   07 06 05 04 03

Library of Congress Cataloging-in-
Publication Data is available upon request.